F*ck Portion Control
FOOD

Nathan Guy Hatch

November 2025

© 2025 Nathan Hatch

Content

Introduction	4	
Important Notes	7	

Breakfasts 8

Yuca Porridge (tapioca)	10
Super Smoothies	12
Invert Sugar	12
Cinnamon Apple Pastry Tart	14
Apple Butter	16
Breakfast Fruit Salad	18
Sweet Potato Pudding	20
Chilaquiles	22
Poached Egg	24
Yuca Hash Browns	24
Fried Egg	26
Sweet Potato Hash Browns	26
Sweet Potato Home Fries	28
Omelette, with Huauzontle	30
Frittata	32
Breakfast Tacos	34
Hollandaise Sauce	36
Spinach Crepes	36
Pesto Eggs	38
Pesto	38
Baked Spinach	40
Breakfast Salad	42
Breakfast Egg and Spinach Salad	44
Breakfast Spinach and Mushrooms	46
Buttered Potatoes	48
Quiche	50
Saturday Morning German Pancake	52
California French Toast	54
Savory Grits	56
Sweet Grits	56
Spelt Groats	58
Oat Groats	58

Lunches 60

Tomatillo Salsa	62
Homemade Corn Chips	62
Sweet Potato Fries	64
Tomatillo Fajitas	66
Baguette	68
Homemade Mayonnaise	70
Easy Pastry Dough	72
Spinach Pastry Tart	74
Mussels and Garlic Tart	76
Cheese and Peaches Tart	78

How to Salad	80
Basic Vinaigrette	81
Basic Salad	81
Peas and Cucumber	82
Sautéed Yam with Salad	84
Brown Sugar, Basil, Lime Fruit Salad	86
Microgreens With Manchego	88
Nachos	90
Refried Beans for Tacos, Burritos, Dip	92
Kabocha Tomatillo Soft Tacos	94
Dinners	**96**
Roast Winter Squash	98
Sautéed Greens	98
Sautéed Green Beans	98
Mashed Yam	98
Pan Roasted Potatoes	100
Roast Chicken or Turkey	102
Pasta	104
Pasta and Mushrooms	106
Pasta with Tomatoes and Garlic	108
Spinach Pasta	110
Curried Cauliflower	112
Stock	114
Corn, Cabbage, and Potato	116
Chicken Soup	118
Garlic Kabocha Soup	120
Split Pea Soup	122
Minestrone	124
White Bean and Mushroom	126
Hearty Cream and Vegetable	128
Garden Greens	130
Black Bean and Red Pepper Stew	132
Cream of Broccoli	134
Bread and Onion Soup	136
Tomato Soup	138
Pork with Purslane and Tomatillos	140
Savory Bread Pudding	142
Broccoli Risotto	144
Mushroom Risotto	146
Pizza	148
Tortillas	150
Pot Pie	152
Pie Dough	152

Introduction

*I am **not** a great cook.* While I grew up with a father who was very talented in the kitchen and produced a wide range of impressive meals he never taught me much about anything, and it was not until living on my own that an absence of culinary skill prevented me not only from eating well but also being healthy and happy, since cooking is one of the most fundamental skills we require for our wellbeing.

Over my twenties I finally learned how to cook from the works of Ina Garten, Martha Stewart, Alton Brown, and from classics like *The Joy of Cooking* and those by Julia Child, and finally learned how to make great food for myself and others.

I also do not cook because I *like* cooking, but because I *like to eat well*, and given to the same kinds of laziness and complacency as most and lacking a natural talent for cooking I appreciate recipes which have a high ratio of result to effort, and the recipes in this book largely seek to produce bountiful meals full of helpful nutrition, to heal the body and mind rather than the exceptionally fancy or labor intensive, and recipes are formulated to provide ample portions either for families or leftovers. If you are single or not large you might want to halve many of the recipes.

Because of my expansive knowledge of health and human biology, most recipes are formulated to achieve maximum compatibility with health in the natural treatment of disease as I understand it, so that this food truly does function as medicine, and while knowledge of biology as discussed in my book *Fuck Portion Control* is required to overcome illness all the recipes in this book directly support wellness in the standard as discussed in my other works.

The silly tradition of dinning with multiple dishes is also part of the problem of poor diets, as there is no requirement in human wellbeing for a meat dish, a carb dish, and a vegetable dish at meals, which was instead a pitiful attempt by the poor and middle class to emulate the rich whom they envy, dinning on several courses prepared by employed professional chefs and teams of staff, which is not at all beneficial to wellbeing as evident by the apparent ill-health of most rich people who suffer the very same mortal limitations as everyone else. Preparing multiple dishes for meals can be time-consuming and expensive so, as what occurred throughout the majority of my upbringing, dishes inadvertently become poor in nutrition to save cost and time rather than making food which is easier to prepare and which can satisfy both nutritional needs *and* palate. There is nothing wrong with having multiple dishes, it just needn't be a priority or requisite, but to instead prioritize the *quality* of every meal.

Additionally, prevalent attitudes about protein also mislead many people into adopting diets which are actually harmful to our health, because while protein is very important it is also a primary target of pathogenic microbes. Even fruit and vegetables do contain protein and amino acids, and protein is not only limited to meat and animal products. Grains, nuts, legumes, and seeds are all quite high in protein too, but also contain protective nutrients like tannins and other polyphenols which, unlike animal products, help protect protein from opportunistic microorganisms which steal protein and amino acids. Our gut microbiome also produces protein (amino acids) from healthy foods, and in a healthy adult eating a healthy diet this is about 20 grams per day, which is quite substantial, and the increase in protein required of aging or metabolic disease is simply the result of pathogenic microbes absconding with our amino acids for their own use, converting them also to things like toxic ammonia, hydrogen sulfide, and biogenic amines like histamine. When blocking pathogens and supporting commensals, the gut microbiome can and will produce a great deal of protein that is also higher quality and a better composition than what is found in most dietary sources. This compliments dietary protein, not replacing it, but dramatically lowers the amount of protein required to be healthy, which can be easily determined simply by cravings and hunger.

When creating this book I inadvertently also discovered how to instinctually shift cravings toward a vegetarian diet rather than one which is heavily anchored in meat. This is achieved by repletion with vitamin D and a diet high in *silicon* as discussed in *Fuck Portion Control*. But this means nearly all the recipes in this book were formulated after experiencing this shift, so most are vegetarian, but can have meat added to them if desired.

This is not an ideological vegetarianism, as the ability to benefit from plant foods is entirely dependent on specific factors like vitamin D and microbial B12, so eating vegetarian without these in place makes a vegetarian diet *less* healthy, not more. Since plants are healthier for us than animal products (but more difficult to digest), restoring the ability to properly digest plant foods is first required to benefit from a diet anchored in plants. Cravings, not ideology, should be used to evaluate these disparities, where strong cravings for meat in preference of vegetables is a primary symptom of vitamin D deficiency (even during sufficient sun exposure), while strong cravings for leafy greens and other fresh plant will occur after vitamin D repletion because vitamin D supplies commensal *Thaumarchaeota* archaea which produce vitamin B12 locally for other commensal microbes to break down plant food in the first place. Work towards achieving the ability to naturally subsist on a primarily vegetarian diet, but *always* use the body and cravings as the guidepost, *not* ideology.

Starchy and sugary plant foods provide far more energy than protein and fats since mitochondrial respiration is driven by carbohydrate, but our commensal microbes also produce an abundance of B vitamins, short chain fatty acids, and protein from indigestible carbohydrates such as what are abundant in plant foods, so meals like a salad can often be more filling than a large dinner of meat and potatoes due to the abundance of microbial activity growing on cellulose and polyphenols, so long as microbes have access to B12. It can sometimes be difficult to restore vitamin D as discussed in *Fuck Portion Control,* so if cravings for plant foods do not naturally exist a supplement of B12 can and should be added to one meal a day (especially those dense in tough plant foods) in order to assist microbes to overcome plant polarity defenses and restore their ability to break them down, which will increase both the nutritional benefit of healthy foods, by liberating the nutrition locked behind plant cell walls, as well as satiation, which is also a function of nutrient repletion.

Because of the toxicity of many agrochemicals it is also best to consume food grown organically as much as possible. Of course, many countries do not require organically labeled food to be 100% organic, and there is much corruption and deceit inherent in food production, so much care should be put into finding and acquiring quality food sources from reputable producers and purveyors. Buying from local market gardeners is often the best strategy, if possible.

But even organic food is not necessarily healthy, since farming methods and practices greatly determine the nutrient density of crops. Selection for yield, size, and resistance to transport and storage, for instance, greatly reduces the nutrient density of foods, with studies showing enormous declines, even over 50%, of vitamin C in produce just over the last several decades. Heritage or heirloom produce, grown through *regenerative*, *no-dig* farming methods which cultivate a robust and healthy soil microbiome results in the most nutritious food possible, and it does not matter if you technically select healthy options at the grocery store it may be impossible to reach levels of requisite nutrition when consuming commercially produced food simply due to the deficit that originates at the farm itself.

Growing your own food, if you have space for a garden, access to a plot, or even some plants in pots if you only have a balcony or window exposure using regenerative principles and heritage or heirloom varieties of plants will produce far higher nutrition to better therapeutically rehabilitate health. This practice will also get you in contact with healthy soil microbes that are also required to recover from many metabolic diseases like diabetes, in addition to achieving sun exposure for vitamin D synthesis.

Cooking can be great fun, but if your culinary skill is limited it can often be an exercise in frustration. If this is the case, use social media to learn and be inspired. Many of us have self-doubts or discouragement when we can't do things like cooking, but this is simply an insecurity borne of childhood neglect or abuse, and practicing inventory as discussed in my other book, *The Perfect Child* can greatly help rehabilitate our self-image to help us accomplish goals such as healthy cooking and eating an being kinder to ourselves when we are reminded of the limitations of mortality.

Of all the life skills we can acquire, cooking is the most essential self-care skill, and while it is wonderful to eat at great restaurants or afford our own personal chefs, no person can be entirely healthy or nurtured without the ability to cook and care for our own wellbeing ourselves. So enjoy these recipes and keep up your good health by taking care of the body and prioritizing your needs, including the acquisition of skills that are be required to do that.

Important Notes

i. The *flavor* of food is *entirely* a consequence of its nutritive profile. For this reason, using highly refined or low nutrient ingredients results in food which is bland. Bleached, white sugar for instance tastes like a chemical and has far less flavor complexity than organic sugar which is not bleached and retains a slight tan color, and fruits and vegetables grown by market gardeners using regenerative practices results in far higher nutrient density and sugar content of plant foods. Choose for *quality* rather than size, bulk, or refinement.

ii. Correctly holding a knife can make the biggest difference in cooking efficiency and safety. Knives are *not* held at the end or middle of the handle, but at the very top, near the blade. This gives the hand maximum leverage and reduces risk of slipping and cutting yourself. Always also keep your knife sharp—every home should have a *whetstone* (the honing steel in your knife set is *not* a sharpener).

iii. Do NOT use garlic mashers. Garlic that is pulverized excessively becomes bitter. Pre-peeled garlic is also treated with chlorine to keep it from browning. Instead, peel your own by smashing cloves with the flat side of a large knife to pop the clove out of the peel.

iv. Seeds contain serotonin to purposefully promote faster gut transit. This can sometimes be useful to reverse constipation, which is caused by opportunistic microbes stealing tryptophan which then promotes excessive water absorption. But consuming high amounts of seeds such as by not seeding a pepper can also result in very uncomfortable, rapid bowel transit, which is not from the heat of the pepper but the serotonin.

i. NEVER put poultry into a preheated oven (especially not a Thanksgiving turkey!)—poultry meat gets heat shock and becomes rubbery. Always put poultry into a cold oven or cold water (if boiling) *before* heating, to slowly bring up the temperature.

ii. Accompany *all* dietary protein, sulfur, and selenium with dietary *carotene* to block harmful reducing microbes. Never mix fluids with protein in the gut unless the fluid contains *tannin* to block microbial ammonia. Dietary oxalate also protects dietary fats from saponification, *though oxalate can result in calcium deficiency if sufficient dietary calcium is not also consumed, generally, and kidney stones if deficient in vitamin D.*

iii. Eggs contain toxic avidin in the egg whites which causes biotin deficiency. *Never* feed soft eggs to children until their microbiome has been well established from months of eating solid food and regular sun exposure. Avidin is heat sensitive so fully-cooked eggs or in foods like pasta or cookies will not cause biotin deficiency.

iv. Never use blade grinders to grind coffee or spices. The spinning blades and high aeration oxidizes the beans or spices. Only use high-quality burr grinders for coffee and a pestle and mortar for spices.

Breakfasts

Yuca Porridge (tapioca)

1-2 whole yuca roots, peeled
pinch salt
½ cup whole milk, half and half, or coconut milk
¼ cup sugar
½ tbsp butter
fruit and cinnamon as desired

Bring a medium pot of water to a boil. After peeling yuca, chop into large pieces and remove the woody center, then add to the boiling water, cook for 40-50 minutes until the yuca is *very* soft. Remove from heat and drain. Add the yuca to blender along with the butter, milk, sugar, and salt and blend briefly until well combined. Serve with cinnamon and fruit or any other mixings as desired.

Yuca is one of the best foods to reset the gut due to its high quantity of carbs, starches, indigestible carbs, oxalate, and cyanide which empowers the immune system. ***Because yuca is high in cyanide, however, it can be poisonous if prepared incorrectly or eaten in excess. Heat inactivates the enzymes which release cyanide, so cooking whole pieces as this recipe directs helps prevent excess. Even so, stop eating if experiencing shortness of breath, which is a symptom of cyanide poisoning.***

Super Smoothies

100 mg plant-sourced silicon
25 mcg selenium
2 cups water
1 tbsp lose tea (green is best)
1 cup fruit juice (grape, orange, lemon, etc).
3-4 cups frozen fruit (berries, peaches, strawberries, etc)
1 scoop pea or casein protein
½ cup sugar (invert sugar if diabetic)
½ cup almonds or 4-5 apricot kernels (for cyanide)
1 tbsp coconut oil, butter, or cocoa butter (melted)

In a small pot add the silicon to the water and bring to a boil, remove from heat and add selenium and tea, steep for 10 minutes. Then in a blender add the tea *with* the tea leaves (they soften during brewing) and all other ingredients. Blend by pulsing slowly to avoid excessive aeration.

*This drink is **not** formulated for children—if making for children greatly reduce tea strength and quantity by more than ½, or use non-caffeinated tea, and DO NOT give apricot kernels to children (keep them out of reach).*

Invert Sugar

2 cups organic sugar
1-2 cups water
½ tsp lemon juice (or ¼ tsp citric acid powder)

In a small pot over high heat bring to a boil. Reduce to low, cover and simmer for ten minutes. Remove from heat and allow to cool before use.

Adding supplements like silicon to water before boiling takes advantage of heat chemistry to make hydrated nutrients which increases their bioavailability (but never boil copper, iron, or manganese as they will oxidize).

The addition of brewed tea leaves adds vitamin K, oxalate, silicon, and more tea tannins than brewing alone, and the oxalates help prevent saponification of the added fat.

Tea obviously adds caffeine to the smoothie, so factor that in your caffeine consumption. Those with low body temperatures should avoid cold beverages like cold smoothies until the metabolic rate is elevated at least somewhat.

Cinnamon Apple Pastry Tart

1 pastry dough (page 72)
4 tbsp butter
2-3 lbs tart apples, sliced horizontally
1 cup sugar (real brown sugar is ideal)
2 tsp cinnamon
4 tbsp butter

Prepare a pastry dough (page 72) while preheating oven to 425°F (220°C), using a baking stone if you have one. *Don't peel or core the apples*, but remove the seeds while slicing. In a small pot melt the butter, cinnamon, and sugar together, then remove from heat. Roll out the pastry dough and fit to a large baking sheet, folding the edges in for a small crust, then bake for 15 minutes until the pastry is puffed and lightly browned. Remove from oven and top with sliced apples laid overlapping each other (pressing down the center), pour the melted butter, cinnamon, and sugar evenly over all the apples then return to oven and bake for another 25 minutes until the apples are soft. Remove from oven and use a pizza wheel or large knife to cut into servings.

The high amount of tannins and polyphenols in apple, apple skin, and cinnamon help to protect the protein and fats in this decadent breakfast treat, while the high quantity of cinnamic acids promote effective ATPase channel function.

Apple Butter

3-4 lbs firm, tart apples (you can use as many as you want, actually, and makes for great preservation), quartered, discard seeds and stems.

1 tsp cinnamon

1 tsp butter

¼ cup water

Cut apples into quarters, discarding seeds and stems. *Do not core*—the core will soften and is the densest source of pectins. Add all ingredients into a very large pot over medium heat. Cover and cook, stirring regularly to prevent burning. The temperature can be lowered as the apples break down, to prevent burning, but will need to cook for several hours (3-4) until apples are well-browned. They must be cooked past the 'apple sauce' stage, as the browning of the sugars is what really makes apple butter so good.

*apple peels do not break down during cooking, but they are very healthy to include due to their high tannin and polyphenol content, and if you don't like the peels you can remove them after cooking or run the apple butter through a food mill to break them down (or you can peel them beforehand but that will remove a lot of potential nutrition). Apple butter is especially delicious served on toast (baguette recipe on page 68), and its high pectins, sugars, and polyphenols help promote a healthy gut microbiome and is a great way to get your microbiome started for the day.

Breakfast Fruit Salad

1 cup heavy whipping cream

1/2 cup sugar

1 cup ricotta cheese (mascarpone would also work)

2-4 lbs fruit, chopped (grapes, pineapple, blackberries, blueberries, strawberries, kiwi, papaya, banana, apple, mandarin oranges, peaches, tangerines, nectarines, etc.)

½ cup hazelnuts or almonds with skins, chopped or ground (use a mortar and pestle or buy pre-ground)

In a large bowl whip the cream and sugar together until the cream is whipped but not beaten to butter. Fold in the ricotta then add the chopped fruit and ground or chopped nuts as desired and mix until well combined, reserving a little of the nuts for decoration on top when serving. Can also be topped with a dusting cinnamon, cocoa powder, or grated chocolate for some more flare if desired. Serves 2-4 people.

The addition of ricotta cheese to this fruit salad adds a dimension not typical of other recipes, and along with the nuts is plenty of protein for a filling breakfast. Including the skins from the nuts also helps inhibit opportunistic gut microbes, although fruit is generally also protective too. While many people think of dietary fat as a liability for the waistline, most hormones are made from fat, so this is actually one of the healthiest breakfasts a person can have.

Sweet Potato Pudding

2 large, orange sweet potatoes, peeled and cubed
4 tbsp butter
¼ tsp salt
3 cups whole milk
1 cup brown sugar
1 tsp tamarind paste
¼ tsp nutmeg

½ tsp cinnamon
4 eggs
1/4 cup flour

Whipped cream (optional):
3/4 cup heavy cream
2 tbsp Sugar

*make this the night before so it's ready by breakfast. Also makes an excellent, healthy dessert.

In a large pan over medium heat melt butter then add sweet potato, salt, and cover, cooking for 25-30 minutes until potatoes are extremely soft, stirring occasionally, *do not brown.* Halfway through cooking, preheat oven to 350°F (175°C) and fill a shallow pan with water and add to lower rack in the oven (to provide steam). When cooked, transfer potatoes to mixing bowl then add the milk, sugar, flour, nutmeg, and tamarind paste and mix until combined using a mixer or potato masher. Last, add the eggs and mix again, then butter a springform cake pan or large soufflé dish, pour in batter and transfer to oven to bake for about 80-90 minutes until center no longer wobbles when disturbed. Remove from oven and allow to rest at least 3-4 hours. Optional: serve with whip cream by beating the cream and sugar together with a mixer or whisk until it forms soft peaks, and serve overtop pudding (garnish with a light dusting of cinnamon if desired).

This sweet potato pudding is an especially indulgent way to feed gut microbes first thing in the morning, and contains an abundance of nutrition. Can be eaten with a dose of lithium to help eradicate gut parasites. Other options for serving include fresh berries or chopped nuts.

Chilaquiles

10-15 corn tortillas (or a bag of corn chips)
1-2 cups coconut oil (or comparable for frying)
1 ½ cup broth (vegetable or chicken)
½ yellow onion, chopped
4-5 high quality tomatoes, chopped
1 jalapeño, chopped, discard seeds
4 cloves garlic, crushed

pinch salt
¼ cup cotija cheese, crumbled
1-2 tbsp Mexican crema or sour cream
1 avocado, cubed or sliced
1 tbsp cilantro or parsley, chopped

In a shallow pan heat coconut oil over medium-high heat. Cut stack of tortillas into 6 by cutting in half, then into thirds. When the oil is hot (you can test by dropping in a slice of tortilla, it should sizzle robustly), fry chips in two or three batches, turning occasionally with two large utensils, until the sizzling slows and the chips are nice and browned but not burnt, remove and set aside (or save yourself time and buy high quality, pre-made chips). Combine the broth, onion, tomatoes, jalapeño, garlic, and salt in a blender and pulse until everything is combined but not overly smooth. Pour sauce into a large pan over medium-high heat, bringing to a simmer and cook about five minutes, stirring occasionally. Add the chips and continue cooking until the sauce is well absorbed and the chips have soaked most of it, also stirring occasionally. Plate the chips then fry an egg or two (page 26) and transfer to the top of the chips, finish with slices of avocado, crumbled cotija cheese, dash of crema or sour cream, and cilantro as desired. Black beans are also a good addition if desired.

Chilaquiles are my absolute favorite breakfast. The salty, chewy, crispy corn chips drowning in a spicy sauce is so, so comforting and the carotene in the tomatoes helps inhibit sulfate and selenate reducing microbes. While cotija cheese may be hard to find there is not really a substitute—it's very salty and flavorful and very unique to Mexican cuisine. Try to get some.

Yuca Hash Browns

1 yuca root, peeled and grated
1 tbsp butter
1 tbsp coconut oil
½ tsp salt
½ tsp ground black pepper
ketchup (optional)

Peel yuca and cut off any hard or woody parts, then grate on the large grate of a cheese grater (never the small grate, which will produce too much cyanide). In a large skillet pan over medium-high heat melt the coconut oil and butter. When the pan is hot and butter sizzling add the shredded yuca, salt, and pepper, mix and spread evenly. Allow to cook on one side for about 6-8 minutes until edges start to brown. Flip yuca once and continue cooking on the other side (do not disturb too frequently otherwise it will get mushy). After the yuca is nicely browned on both sides remove and plate. Top with poached or fried egg, ketchup, or tomato. Season with additional pinch of salt and pepper.

Poached Egg

1-2 eggs (per person)
2 tbsp vinegar
pinch salt
pinch ground black pepper

Fill a small pot halfway with water, add the vinegar and a pinch of salt, then bring to a simmer (the salt and vinegar helps keep the whites constrained). Crack one egg and gently slip it into the water, cook for 2-3 minutes until the white is opaque, using a butter knife to gently twirl the whites together. Remove using a slotted spoon, salt and pepper after plating.

Poaching an egg only denatures about 75% of its avidin, so it's safer but not entirely safe for young children or those with gut problems.

The whole yuca root is much healthier than when refined to flour or starch (tapioca) because it contains useful cyanide to support the immune system (which is otherwise lost during processing). Many young people easily recover from gut dysbiosis, bloating, and weight gain simply from eating yuca regularly. High in starch and other nutrients it also makes for a very satisfying hash brown, and taken with a dose of lithium can help combat gut parasites. I often eat this without the egg, with ketchup. Remember that yuca can be high in cyanide and poisonous if eaten in excess.

Sweet Potato Hash Browns

½ large sweet potato (or 1 small), peeled and grated
1 tsp paprika
½ tsp garlic powder (or minced fresh garlic)
¼ tsp salt
¼ tsp ground black pepper
2 tbsp butter
ketchup (optional)

In a large pan over medium heat, melt the butter. While the butter is melting mix the grated sweet potato, paprika, garlic powder, salt, and pepper in a bowl until well combined. Once the butter is no longer bubbling add the sweet potato and spread around the pan in an even layer. Allow to cook for about 3-4 minutes at a time, stirring occasionally to evenly cook, for about 15 minutes until the potato is nicely browned. When approaching the end do not stir as often, instead flip the entire portion like a pancake to evenly sear the outsides. When the potato is well browned remove from heat and plate. Top browns with the egg and a pinch of salt and pepper on the eggs. Serve with ketchup.

Fried Egg

1-2 eggs (per person)
pat of butter
pinch salt
pinch ground pepper

Add a little butter to a hot pan and crack the eggs in, careful not to break the yolk. Salt and pepper, then cover with a lid and cook until the whites are browned at the edges, fully set, but the yolk is still wobbly. DO NOT OVERCOOK.

Frying an egg only reduces its avidin by 50%, so it too is not technically safe for young children or those with severe gut or metabolic problems

Root vegetables are the fastest way to a healthy gut, and having something like sweet potato daily for breakfast, especially with a small dose of supplemental lithium, can ensure plenty of butyric acid synthesis by our friendly microbes which is required for functions like the uptake of iodine, lithium, sodium, or activation of vitamin D.

Sweet Potato Home Fries

1 large sweet potato (or 2 small), peeled and cubed
½ tsp salt
1 tsp paprika
½ tsp garlic powder (or minced garlic)
¼ tsp ground black pepper
3-4 tbsp butter or coconut oil
Ketchup (optional)

In a large pan over medium heat, melt the butter, then add the potato, salt, and cover. Cook for 10 minutes, stirring occasionally to prevent sticking, then add the rest of the spices, toss, cover again and cook another 10 minutes (it can take up to 25 minutes for sweet potato to soften sufficiently—be patient, don't turn up the heat or you'll get a stuck on mess. Serve with ketchup and other breakfast fare if desired.

One of the easiest and most healthful breakfasts, roots like sweet potato or yam are an ideal and delicious way to start your microbiome for the day, eaten with a small dose of lithium can help evict gut parasites.

Omelette, with Huauzontle

2-3 stalks Huauzontle, trimmed
4 eggs
2 tbs olive or coconut oil
3 tbs butter
salt
soft, mild cheese (mozzarella, provolone, etc.)

toppings (as desired):
sour cream
avocado
hot sauce

First, trim the huauzontle of all hard stems (discard). In a small pan over medium heat add the oil and 1 tbsp butter, then add the huauzontle and a pinch of salt, sauté for about 10 minutes. Remove from heat and set aside. While the huauzontle is cooking break the eggs into a small bowl, add a pinch of salt and scramble until well combined (I am not good at making omelettes even when I do it the way you're supposed to, as you can see from the photo, lol, so if you have a better method, use it). Then, in the same small pan add the remaining butter and when it stops sizzling add the eggs and let cook until they stop bubbling and begin to dry out on the top. Lay the cheese flat on the egg in the center, add the huauzontle on top, and let the egg continue cooking (you can lower the heat to prevent burning) until the cheese starts to melt. Using a spatula, upturn the sides of the omelette over the filling, then slide out of a pan onto the serving plate, flipping the omelette over in the process. Garnish with toppings as desired.

Huauzontle (haw-wa-zon-til-lay) is an extremely nutritious and delicious plant native to the Americas that resembles broccoli in texture and flavor. It is very, very high in oxalate however, which can make it a problem for those deficient in vitamin D but great for helping to protect calcium from opportunistic microbes and prevent the saponification of dietary fats, making it useful for restoration of cholesterol production when served with dietary fat. If you don't have access to huauzontle, use another high oxalate food like spinach.

Frittata

5 eggs
2 crowns of broccoli, diced (or other vegetables of your choosing)
4-5 cloves of garlic, peeled and diced
½ cup grated cheese (mozzarella, parmesan, etc.)
½ tsp salt
½ tsp black pepper
3 tbsp butter

Preheat oven to 350° F (175°C). In a large pan over medium heat sauté the broccoli and garlic with only 2 tbsp of the butter and a little water (to add steam). Meanwhile, scramble the eggs in a bowl, adding the grated cheese to mix well. Put 2/3 of the salt and pepper in the broccoli, the other 1/3 in the eggs. Then melt the remaining 1 tbsp butter in a small omelet pan (or medium pan), and when the broccoli is bright green and soft transfer to small pan, top with the eggs, spreading evenly, then cook over medium-low heat until the edges of the eggs just start to firm up and the center bubbles slightly. Change oven to *high broil*, then transfer to oven for about 5 minutes until the top of the frittata is lightly browned. Serve with sour cream, chives, hot sauce, avocado, etc.

*frittata has one of the easiest impressiveness to effort ratio of any meal, and takes only about ten minutes to put together. Any vegetable can be substituted, but using a source of vitamin K like broccoli or spinach makes this an easy way to get vitamin K and xanthophylls early in the daytime before sun exposure. Adding or substituting with huauzontle or other high-oxalate food can promote better digestion of the fats than broccoli by preventing saponification, since broccoli is very low in oxalate and will not provide that benefit. Potato frittata is also nice.

Breakfast Tacos

1 cup red cabbage, sliced very thin
4 corn tortillas
2 tbsp butter
4-5 eggs
3 tsp vinegar

1 tsp sugar
2 pinches salt
½ cup good cheese
hot sauce (optional)
sour cream (optional)

First, make the cabbage in small bowl by combining cabbage, 2 tsp vinegar, sugar, and pinch of salt. Stir and set aside. Then, heat a large pan over high heat and when hot grill tortillas 30 seconds on each side (reduce to medium-high to prevent excess smoking) then set aside and remove pan from heat. Mix the remaining vinegar (1 tsp) into the eggs before scrambling to neutralize some of the avidin, then scramble with a pinch of salt. Add butter to the pan back over medium heat, when the sizzling slows add the eggs and cook, moving constantly to prevent burning and sticking, until they coalesce but are not dry. Remove from heat and assemble tacos with egg first then cabbage, cheese, hot sauce, sour cream, or any other desired toppings like avocado, radish, cilantro, etc.

Because eggs do not have any protective phytonutrients to guard against opportunistic microbes, the use of high polyphenol toppings like red cabbage can help make this breakfast safer. Although vinegar helps neutralize the avidin in egg whites it will not get all of it and this only helps reduce the harmful effect of avidin, not eliminate it, which only happens when eggs are fully cooked such as hard-boiled or in baked goods.

Spinach Crepes

1 cup flour
1 cup milk, room temperature
½ cup water
2 large eggs
3 tbsp melted butter *(not hot!)*
½ tsp salt
1 package frozen spinach
extra butter

First, preheat a large pan over medium heat. Then in a medium bowl mix the flour, warm milk, warm water, eggs, and a pinch of salt. Lightly butter the pan, then spoon a ladle of batter into the pan and cook until the top of the crepe dries out and the underside is nice and brown (about 2-3 minutes). Flip and cook the other side for 1 more minute. Stack crepes as they finish. When the crepes are done, add the spinach, a pinch of salt, and 2 tbsp of butter to the pan and cook until spinach is no longer watery. While the spinach cooks, prepare the hollandaise sauce. Assemble crepes by wrapping or folding with spinach inside, then pour hollandaise over crepes and serve.

Hollandaise Sauce

2 egg yolks
1 tbsp lemon juice
8 tbsp butter, melted and very hot
pinch cayenne pepper
pinch salt

In a small bowl whisk together the egg yolks, lemon juice, cayenne, and salt. When the spinach is done, spoon into crepes (roll or fold as you like) and plate. Heat the butter on the stove until it is lightly bubbling, then slowly dribble into the yolks, whisking vigorously. When all the butter is incorporated keep whisking until it thickens (about 45-60 seconds). Use immediately (does not store well).

Hollandaise takes all of five minutes to make, so don't let this dish intimidate you because it's one of the healthiest meals you can eat. If using fresh spinach, first immerse in water to remove its nitrates, which will reduce the chances of having a migraine or promoting microbial avidin producers.

Pesto Eggs

4 eggs
1 tsp vinegar (optional)
½ tsp ground black pepper
pinch salt
1 tbsp butter
½ cup pesto

In a small bowl mix the eggs and vinegar to neutralize the avidin, then add the salt and pepper and mix. In a small pan over medium heat melt the butter, then add the eggs. Stir infrequently but enough to keep the eggs from browning. When the eggs are almost done add the pesto and only mix lightly, to prevent blending. Remove from heat and serve with toasted baguette (page 68).

Pesto

3-4 cups fresh basil, finely chopped
4-5 cloves garlic, peeled and crushed
½ tsp salt
¼ cup nuts (pine nuts are preferred, but hazelnuts and walnuts work well too)
¼ cup high quality hard cheese (parmesan, romano, manchego, etc.)
½ cup high quality olive oil

Grind ingredients one at a time in a large mortar until pesto is smooth and combined. You can use a blender, which is far easier, but it's not quite the same. Add a very small pinch of salt with each ingredient to help break down faster. Grind basil leaves last, in batches since they all won't fit at a time, adding more leaves as the previous batch shrinks. Mix everything together in a bowl, with the olive oil. If you have a large mortar all the ingredients can be processed at once.

*Pesto is an **indulgent** way to get vitamin K and xanthophylls, although scrambled eggs are not the safest and should be avoided by very young children or anyone with severe metabolic disease until improvement is made.*

Baked Spinach

1 lb frozen spinach (or 2-3 lbs fresh), chopped
1 yellow onion, minced
5-6 garlic cloves, minced
1 tsp olive oil
2 cups bread crumbs
1 cup heavy cream
2 eggs
1 cup hard cheese (such as parmesan, romano, etc.)
1 tsp ground pepper
½ tsp salt

Preheat oven to 400°F (200° C). In a small, oven-safe pan sauté onions and garlic in olive oil over medium heat, about 10 minutes until soft and translucent. Add spinach and cook until most of the water is removed, then set aside and allow to cool. In a large bowl add eggs, cream, salt, pepper, cheese, and bread crumbs (reserve ½ cup of bread crumbs for the top) and mix until well combined. Add the cooled spinach and onions and garlic and mix again. Pour everything into the pan, top with remaining breadcrumbs, then place in the oven and bake for 20-25 minutes until the spinach is set and the top starts to brown. Change oven to broil for 5 minutes to create a nice even crust at the top (do not burn!). Remove from oven and allow to cool for about 10 minutes before serving. *Be very cautious of hot handle (turn away from front of stove to avoid grabbing).*

Greens for breakfast provides necessary xanthophylls for the synthesis of vitamin D from sun exposure to the skin during the day. Greens also contain vitamin K which not only helps us metabolize calcium but promotes good gut microbes. Other greens like chard, collards, or kale could also substitute if desired, but are low in oxalates which can result in saponification of the fats in the cream and butter in those with gut and metabolic problems.

Breakfast Salad

Per person:
2 slices bread, toasted (baguette, page 68)
2-3 cups baby spinach
1 cup small tomatoes, halved
2 eggs, poached or fried (pages 22, 24)
½ cup good cheese, shredded

½ lemon vinaigrette recipe (page 81)
1 clove garlic
pinch salt
pinch ground pepper

Make poached or fried eggs (pages 22 and 24) while toasting the bread. Make ½ the recipe of a lemon vinaigrette per person (page 81) in a medium bowl with the clove of minced garlic (I prefer using a lemon vinaigrette in the mornings since it's more refreshing than vinegar), then add the spinach to the dressing and toss, add the salt, pepper, tomatoes, and cheese. Plate the slices of bread topped with the salad and eggs, garnish with a pinch of additional ground pepper.

While spinach isn't often considered a breakfast food, we require xanthophyll carotenoids to produce vitamin D, so having greens in the morning is much more useful than later in the day. The acid of the salad dressing can also help neutralize the avidin in the egg whites, which is also mostly inactivated (about 70%) during poaching.

Breakfast Egg and Spinach Salad

4-5 eggs
3 tbsp good olive oil
1 tbsp coconut oil
juice of 1 lemon (or ¼ cup vinegar)
1 tsp ground black pepper

1 tsp sugar
1 tbsp wet mustard
1 tsp dried dill (optional)
3-4 cups baby spinach, *chiffonade*
pinch salt

First, set a small pot over high heat, ¾ full of water with the eggs to slowly bring up their temperature to boiling. Once water is boiling, continue for 6 minutes. Remove from heat but allow to continue cooking for about 10 minutes. Drain eggs and put under cold water to cool rapidly, remove shells. While the eggs are boiling making the vinaigrette by mixing the oil, lemon or vinegar, pepper, sugar, dill, and mustard and whisking until thickened. After eggs are boiled, cooled, and peeled, chop roughly then add to vinaigrette, mix, then add the spinach and salt and mix again. Serve with toast if desired. Prepare the night before for meal prep if your mornings are too busy.

Hard boiling eggs is the best way to inactivate their avidin content. The high silicon and oxalate of the spinach help promote good cholesterol production from the fat (by preventing saponification), which is also required for vitamin D and hormone synthesis.

Breakfast Spinach and Mushrooms

3 tbsp butter
3 tbsp coconut oil (or another 3 tbsp butter)
1-2 packages (about 1-2 cups) mushrooms, sliced
4 cloves garlic, smashed and chopped
½ tsp salt
2 cups frozen spinach or 4 cups fresh.

If using fresh spinach, immerse in water for a few minutes to help remove some of the nitrate (frozen spinach is pre-washed), then drain and set aside. In a medium pan or pot over medium-high heat sauté the mushrooms in the butter, coconut oil, and salt until they start to release their liquid. Add the garlic and continue cooking until the mushrooms are only slightly shrunken. Add the spinach and continue cooking, stirring, for about 8-10 minutes until most of the liquids are cooked off. Serve with good bread, eggs, or other breakfast fare.

There is something about the combination of spinach and mushrooms which feels acceptably breakfasty, and the spinach supplies the daily needed xanthophyll, vitamin K, and oxalate to protect the fat while the large amount of garlic also helps provide necessary dietary sulfur which is in turn protected from hydrogen sulfide producers by the carotene in the spinach.

Buttered Potatoes

per person:
2 large potatoes, peeled and sliced thin
1-2 eggs
2 tbsp butter
½ tsp salt
1 tsp ground black pepper

Melt the butter in a large skillet over medium heat, then add the potatoes, salt, and pepper. Stir to coat, then cover and allow to cook for 15-20 minutes until the potatoes are soft when pierced with a fork, turning potatoes every couple minutes to ensure even cooking. When the potatoes are done remove from pan and plate. Fry each egg in the remaining butter for about 4 minutes, covering quickly so the trapped steam helps cook the top while the base is fried, and season with salt and pepper (the egg is done as soon as the top becomes cloudy). Do not overcook, or the inside won't be runny. When the egg is done place on top of potatoes and serve.

I made this recipe as a way to get soft, delicious, fast potatoes for breakfast. Potato is high in potassium and carbs, with a small amount of keto acids our body can use to make protein, a process that also sequesters ammonia, and a small amount of oxalate which helps protect the fat from saponification. Sliced tomatoes make a great side.

Quiche

1 pie dough (page 150)
1 head garlic, peeled and minced
4-5 bay leaves
2 tsp ground black pepper
6 eggs
1 quart heavy cream
2 tsp salt
1 cup good cheese like parmesan, goat, etc.

choose 2-4 vegetables for the filling, such as:
1 large leek, sliced thin
4 large shallots, peeled and sliced thin
2 large potatoes, cubed
1 head of broccoli, chopped
1 cup of spinach, chopped
2 medium turnips, cubed
1 bunch asparagus, chopped
3 parsnips, cubed small
1 fennel bulb, cubed small
4-5 leaves of collard greens, chopped

for brunch or parties make the day before and refrigerate, bring to room temperature 1 hour before serving

Sauté vegetables in a little butter with the minced garlic, salt, pepper, and bay leaf. Vegetables will not cook in the filling, so cook them fully, a little browning is nice. Set aside to cool, remove bay leaves.

Preheat oven to 350°F (175°C). Make the pie dough (page 146), then roll dough on a floured surface to fit a springform pan or pie tin (my springform pan is 8 inch but 9 inch are more common) and carefully roll the dough over a rolling pin to transfer and form the dough to the pan. If using a springform pan *do not cut overhanging dough* or it will sink when baking, but do mold the edges to be even. In a pie tin crimp edges to a fluted, high pattern around the edges to deepen quiche. Prick the base of dough to prevent air bubbles (you can use pie weights but I don't usually find them necessary). Bake the pie crust for 15-20 minutes until it is just starting to brown. Remove from oven and set aside to cool.

In a large bowl mix eggs, cream, salt, cheese, and mix until combined then mix with the vegetables and cook in a large pan over medium, stirring constantly, until the filling begins to thicken (this will prevent soggy crust and oven spills). When thickened, pour into crust. For a springform pan, cut extra crust from the top. If using a pie dish, brush crust with a little cream or egg wash to make it shiny, then rip 2-inch wide strips of aluminum foil and cover crust to prevent burning. Bake for 35 minutes until top is lightly browned and the center no longer wobbles, removing aluminum covers 10 minutes before it's done. Remove from oven and allow to set and cool at least 2 hours before serving.

Quiche is the rare dish that is entirely worth the time and effort, especially on a nice weekend when there is ample time to make brunch. There is nothing I hate more than a shallow quiche, though. I prefer to make it in a springform pan which allows for very deep pieces and easy removal and impressive, self-standing crust.

This particular quiche is parsnip, fennel, and collard greens.

*EVERYONE GETS BURNED BY THE HANDLE WHEN MAKING THIS DISH! TURN THE HANDLE AWAY FROM PEOPLE TO AVOID INJURY! LEAVING HANDLE TURNED OUTWARD IS AN INVITATION TO GRAB.

Saturday Morning German Pancake

1 cup white flour
1 cup whole milk
1/2 tsp salt
6 eggs
1 stick (1/2 cup) butter

Optional Apple Compote:
2-3 apples peeled, cubed small
1/2 cup sugar
1 tbsp cinnamon
6 tablespoons butter
Pinch of salt

Preheat oven to 350° F (175° C). Place a large, oven-safe skillet or pan on the stove over medium heat, add butter and melt, remove from heat when melted (do not burn or cook). In a large bowl combine milk, salt, and eggs until well combined, then add the flour and combine until smooth. Allow to rest several minutes so the flour properly absorbs the liquid, then stir again before pouring batter into center of melted butter. If making the apple compote, place large dollops around the pan, then place into oven and bake for 30 minutes until sides are risen high and browned. Serve immediately with a dusting of powdered sugar.

For compote, add all ingredients to a medium sauce pan, cook on medium heat for 15 minutes or until apples are barely soft. After batter is poured into the pan, add compote onto batter in dollops before cooking, *do not mix*.

Sometimes you just have to start the weekend with a decadent, indulgent breakfast, and German pancakes are absolutely that. Some recipes have weird cooking instructions though, but making a German pancake couldn't be any simpler, delicious, and healthy when made with these ingredients. If you've never made this before it's quite a spectacular sight when you first take it out of the oven—but it quickly deflates so make sure your family or sweetheart is nearby to witness your amazingness when you pull it out. Pairs well with sausages and coffee.

California French Toast

4-8 slices of brioche or other French bread, 1-inch thick
1 cup corn cereal, crushed to ¼ inch crumbs
1 cup whole milk
2 eggs
pinch salt
1 tsp cinnamon
4 tbsp butter
1 cup apricot jam (or maple syrup)

On a large plate spread the corn cereal and use the bottom of a mug or jar to gently crush the cereal into crumbs. Next, in a large bowl combine the eggs, milk, pinch of salt, and cinnamon and blend with a whisk until everything is well combined. Set a large pan over medium heat and melt the butter, then take one or two slices of bread at at time, dunk into the milk batter, allow to soak for a moment, then dip into corn flakes, transfer to the pan, and cook each side about 5 minutes until corn is gently browned. Dilute apricot jam with about ¼ cup of water and microwave or heat on the stove so it is runny and syrupy, serve over french toast (cold maple syrup or other syrup is also great). Pairs well with sausages or bacon.

This recipe is my Father's, and we grew up having 'California' French toast many a weekend breakfast (this is best with light, fluffy, french style bread such as brioche which I did not have at the time making, and yours will turn out much better than the photo on the right if you use better bread). Adding a lot of spice to the batter such as cinnamon helps inhibit some opportunistic microbes, and the use of real apricot or maple syrup helps as well.

Savory Grits

2 cups wet-packed hominy (canned)
1 pasilla pepper, seeded and minced
2 tbsp butter
pinch salt
½ tsp ground black pepper
½ cup soft cheese, shredded (cheddar, mozzarella, etc)
¼ cup whole milk

Sweet Grits

2 cups wet-packed hominy (canned)
pinch salt
2 tbsp butter
1 tbsp honey
¼ cup whole milk

In a blender add the hominy along with its canning liquid (if you don't have a blender use a potato masher while cooking the hominy to mash it), pulse until it is coarsely ground (this only works with wet-pack hominy). Then in a small pot over medium heat sauté the diced pasilla pepper in butter with the salt and pepper for 5 minutes. Add the ground hominy (and a little water if it is too thick), bring to a simmer then cover, cooking for 20 minutes, stirring every few minutes to prevent burning. Remove from heat, add a tab more butter and the cheese, allow to melt, then add whole milk as desired. Alternatively grits can be made sweet, using honey and butter (added after cooking the corn) instead of peppers and cheese.

Corn must be nixtamalized (treated with an alkali) in order to be digestible, but most corn products are not, especially commercial grits, so grits are much healthier when made from hominy (which is corn treated with lime—not the fruit lime, but calcium hydroxide, as in limestone). When using peppers like pasilla it is also important to remove the seeds, not because they are hot but because seeds actually contain high amounts of serotonin which causes faster gut transit and so reduces digesting time and sometimes discomfort.

Spelt Groats

1 cup whole spelt berries
2 cups water
pinch salt

optional: butter, milk, sugar, berries, cinnamon

Oat Groats

1 cup whole oat berries
2 cups water
pinch salt

A full day before cooking, combine spelt or oats with the water in a small bowl or container, cover and leave on the counter or other room-temperature spot to soak. Water activates the enzyme *phytase* in the grains which breaks down the anti-nutrient *phytate,* while useful tannins leach into the soaking water, so *do not* dump the water the next day. Instead, transfer everything to a blender (optional) and pulse to roughly chop some of the grain, then transfer to a small pot over medium-high heat, add the pinch of salt and bring to a boil then cover and reduce to a very low simmer for about 45 minutes until all of the water is absorbed and the grains are soft. It will tend to boil over the first ten minutes, so keep and eye on it, and stir occasionally to prevent burning. Serve with a pat of butter, whole milk, sugar, berries, or cinnamon as desired.

While groats take a full 25 hours to prepare, it is low effort and only requires some planning ahead. This meal is one of the best ways to get more vitamin E, which helps to treat conditions like asthma and so-called 'autoimmunity' by inhibiting oxidation chain reactions. But whole grain is difficult to digest and requires soaking for at least 24 hours to break down phytate and increase vitamin E by about 50-100%. Grain can be sprouted even longer if desired for even more vitamin E and greater digestibility. Whole grain should never be eaten unless it is sprouted or fermented.

Lunches

Tomatillo Salsa

4 lbs tomatillos, husked and washed
1 large onion, chopped rough
2 jalapeños, halved and seeded
1 head garlic, smashed and peeled
½ tsp salt
juice of ½ lime
1 bunch cilantro

In a large pan over medium-high heat, add the whole tomatillos, onion, jalapeños, garlic, and salt, cover and allow to scorch slightly on all sides, turning occasionally, for about 8-10 minutes until tomatillos burst and are soft. Remove from heat, allow to cool, then add to a blender with the cilantro and blend smooth. Serve with chips, on tacos, etc., and store leftovers in the fridge.

Homemade Corn Chips

1 package soft corn tortillas (make sure they contain 'lime' in the ingredients, or 'nixtamalized')
½ lb coconut oil
salt

In a deep, wide pot heat the coconut oil until it just starts smoking (turn down the heat if smoking too much). Add about ¼ tsp salt to the oil. While the oil is heating cut stack of tortillas into 1/6 wedges (cut in half, then each half into thirds). When the oil is hot immediately and *carefully* add chips to the hot oil, spreading around with a metal, slotted spoon. Don't overcrowd. Cook in batches, turning chips after about 2 minutes on each side. When chips are lightly brown remove using slotted spoon and metal strainer. Dump into large bowl or platter and immediately sprinkle with a pinch of salt. Serve with salsa, bean dip (page 92), or other Mexican fare.

***Always use extreme caution when frying foods. Hot oil can combust or cause injury if spilled. Never put out an oil fire with water—turn off the heat source, cover, and use a fire extinguisher.

Sweet Potato Fries

1 sweet potato per person (white or orange), peeled and cut into strips
1 lb coconut oil
1 tsp salt

In a large pan place the coconut oil and salt over high heat until the oil gets very hot but is not smoking (lower the temperature slightly if smoking excessively). Adding the salt to the oil instead draws the water out of the fries, which vaporizes in the hot oil, and helps produce a crispy fry without the need to par boil. When the oil is hot, add the fries about 1 potato's worth at a time (crowding the pan too much can cause longer cooking times). Using a slotted spoon, occasionally turn the fries until they are nicely and evenly browned but not close to burning. Using a slotted spoon and a strainer, carefully remove fries without splashing oil. When the fries are removed sprinkle with a pinch of salt and serve with ketchup or as a side to sandwiches, salads, or other fare.

BE VERY CAREFUL WHEN FRYING FOODS, as hot oil can easily combust into flames or hurt people if spilled—if you have children, always turn the handle away from the front of the stovetop when frying. If hot oil catches fire do NOT use water to put it out. Instead, turn off the heat source, cover flames with a lid, and use fire a commercial extinguisher.

Frying normally calls for par-boiling, but that also causes leaching of potassium, and simply adding some salt to the cooking oil helps crisp fries a bit without requiring that step. As regular potatoes contain solanine which contributes to alcoholism, choosing sweet potatoes for fries can be a great, indulgent option for those in recovery or have other neurological problems. Fried foods are also not unhealthy because they're fried, they are unhealthy because of the types of oil used. Frying in stable fats like coconut oil turn foods like fries and doughnuts into health foods rich in nutrition.

Tomatillo Fajitas

1 lb tomatillos, hulled
5-6 red bell peppers, seeded and sliced chunky
2 onions, peeled and large cubed
4-6 corn tortillas per person, grilled
Optional toppings like cheese, guacamole or avocado, salsa and hot sauce, cilantro, sour cream, etc.

First, grill the tortillas on a hot pan, about 30 seconds on each side, then set aside. Then in the same, hot pan add the tomatillos, onions, and peppers. They will squeak and sizzle, allow to char by not stirring frequently, but try to keep all the tomatillos touching the hot pan as they take the longest to cook. Stir occasionally, reducing the heat a little if it starts to get smokey, until the tomatillos just start to break open. Remove from heat and serve with tortillas and toppings as desired.

Fajitas are so easy to make and this dish is full of carotene and other good nutrition, and pan frying tomatillos, onions, and peppers together on a hot pan is one of the most aromatic experiences cooking can offer.

Baguette

6 cups white flour (spelt, einkorn, kamut, etc.)
2 ½ cups water
1 tsp dry active yeast
1 tsp salt

The night before baking add the flour, water, yeast, and salt to a large bowl, put the salt in a different spot than the yeast(so it doesn't kill the yeast). Allow the yeast to bloom in the water for about five minutes, then mix everything with a stiff wooden spoon or stand mixer. When combined, turn out onto a clean surface and knead by pushing the dough away from you, rolling back on itself, and repeating that motion for about 6-8 minutes until the dough is entirely smooth (doesn't really matter how you knead, just do it). When the dough is smooth you're done kneading. Return to bowl, cover, and leave on the counter overnight (8-10 hours—can be done before work too, and then bake when you get home).

The next day, flour a baking sheet (or use parchment), then turn out the dough onto a countertop and cut into two pieces using a dough scraper or sharp knife. Flatten and roll each piece until you feel the gluten stiffen and the dough is harder to stretch, then flatten again into a medium-sized rectangle, roll up lengthwise into a cylinder, then roll the ends slightly thinner than the middle. Transfer to floured baking sheet, but *do not* cover dough, as the weight of a towel will cause flattening (if you own a baker's couche and transfer boards you can of course use those). Allow to rise for about 1 hour or until dough is risen about 50% larger.

30 minutes before baking preheat oven to 450°F (230°C). Then fill a large, oven safe pan about halfway with water and bring to a boil on the stovetop, then *very carefully* transfer to the lowest rack in the oven for steam (if you can't do this put the water pan directly in the oven and let it preheat longer—it's better to be safe!). When oven is heated score the baguettes using a razor blade, with a long slash off-center down the entire length or three or four diagonal slashes, holding the blade at a 45° angle rather than cutting straight into the dough (the point is to cut the skin and not the interior, which then lifts up into a nice crunchy "ear" during cooking). Finally, transfer dough to oven and bake for 30-35 minutes until bread is well-browned. Remove from oven and allow to rest at least 10 minutes before opening (you can also bake with bread pans—use parchment to prevent sticking).

While many people are allergic to gluten this reaction actually takes place in the lower intestine from opportunistic microbes feeding on tough, undigested gluten and added iron in common wheat. Gluten in ancient grains like spelt, einkorn, and kamut is more easily digested, and in the many years I have been eating ancient grains have never had a stomachache or allergic reaction as occurred with common wheat.

Baguette bread is great for breakfasts, snacks, and sandwiches or to accompany salads, soup, and other light fare. While this recipe and technique would not meet professional bakery standards it's great for amateur, home cooks to get bread as easy as possible (and this recipe is indeed very easy). Spelt tends to get a crunchier crust than other grains (especially in dry climates), but storing in a bag or container will cause the crust to soften considerably. Baguette is especially delicious with some room-temperature, high quality butter.

Whole grain spelt can be substituted for white flour but in which case about ¼ cup more water should be added to the recipe. Or one or two cups of whole grain can be substituted for white for some additional nutrients. A sourdough starter can also be used instead of dry active yeast, just add a little more flour if it's too wet and it might require 5-10 minutes longer in the oven.

Homemade Mayonnaise

2 egg yolks
juice of ½ lemon
splash of vinegar (apple cider is great, but any will do)
pinch of salt
½ tsp mustard (wet or dry)
2 cups high-oleic sunflower oil

Allow eggs to come to room temperature before using (you can run them under warm water to speed that up). Then add all ingredients except for the oil to a small or medium bowl and whisk until well combined (this can be done by hand or an electric hand mixer but *not* a blender). Slowly begin to drizzle oil in a steady stream, ½ cup at a time, allowing the oil to be fully incorporated into the emulsion before adding more. Mayonnaise is famous for 'splitting' (falling apart), and the key to avoid this is *time,* because the longer oil is acidified by the lemon and vinegar the more it will hold to the emulsion, so you can even take a break for a minute or two inbetween each ½ cup of oil to let the oil acidify and stabilize (which will also give your arm rest). Once all the oil is incorporated immediately put into a jar and refrigerate. Homemade mayonnaise does not last very long (up to two weeks), so make use of it on sandwiches, salad dressing, avocado toast, etc.

Oleic acid stabilizes our primary respiratory enzyme, cytochrome oxidase, so the use of this mayonnaise can actually rehabilitate mitochondrial respiration and directly raise the metabolic rate, so long as saponification of fats in the gut is prevented (acid emulsion in the mayonnaise already helps with this), and thus the use of high-oleic sunflower oil in this mayonnaise not only produces a smooth and delicious product but is also very nutritious.

Easy Pastry Dough

2.5 cups flour (spelt, einkorn, or kamut)
1 cup cold water
½ tsp salt
8 tbsp cold butter

Mix the flour, salt, and water until fully combined. Turn out and briefly knead until dough is smooth but don't overwork, then allow to rest for 10-15 minutes. Next, on a floured worktop roll dough into a medium sized rectangle. Cut cold butter into 6 strips lengthwise and arrange side by side (long sides touching) into a flat layer on ½ of the dough only. Fold the other half of dough over the butter, seal the edges, and form into a nice rectangle (the more uniform the better the result).

Place in the refrigerator for 5-6 minutes so the temperature of the butter and dough equalize, then remove from fridge and roll dough into a rectangle twice its size, fold by thirds from the short side, one side first then other on top (as pictured above). Repeat this step 3 more times. After 4-5 total turns the dough is ready to be used.

If at any time the butter squishes in the pastry it is too warm and should be put into the fridge for 5-10 minutes but not so long that the butter hardens—If dough cracks when rolling it's too cold, leave to rest for a few minutes to warm before proceeding.

Pastry is way easier than you think, and lots of fun to work with.

Spinach Pastry Tart

1 pastry dough (page 72)
4 tbsp butter
1 large yellow onion, minced
1 head garlic, peeled and minced
1 tsp salt
1 tsp ground black pepper

1 lb frozen spinach, fully thawed
1 cup breadcrumbs
2 eggs (reserve one for egg wash)
2 cups good cheese (parmesan, manchego, etc.), finely shredded

Prepare a pastry dough (page 72) while preheating oven to 425°F (220°C), using a baking stone if you have one. Make the filling by first sautéing the onions in the butter and salt until they are translucent and just starting to brown, adding garlic and pepper halfway through. When the onions are done add the spinach and cook an additional 6-8 minutes to remove most of the water, then set aside to cool. Lightly dust a baking sheet with flour, then roll dough the size of the sheet and transfer, fold the edges over to create a small rim, prick the surface with a fork, and place dough in oven and bake for 20 minutes until it is puffed and browning. While the pastry is cooking combine the remaining ingredients with the spinach and onions (reserve 1 egg and scramble with 1 tsp water for egg wash), and when the pastry is cooked remove from oven, top with spinach, brush edges with egg wash, and return to oven to cook an additional 20 minutes until the edges are golden brown. Remove from oven and cut into servings using a pizza cutter. Can be made into individual tarts if desired.

This spinach tart is an indulgent way to get your vitamin K, silicon, calcium, fats, protein, and sulfur.

Mussels and Garlic Tart

1 pastry dough (page 72)
8 cloves garlic, rough chopped
1 1/2 cups mussel meat (smoked are best), chopped
1/4 tsp salt
1/2 tsp pepper

1 tbsp thyme
1 cup breadcrumbs
1 cup parmesan, grated
½ cup fresh parsley, minced
1 egg

Prepare a pastry dough (page 72), while preheating the oven to 425°F (220°C), using a baking stone if you have one. Make the filling by mixing all the remaining ingredients in a medium bowl (reserve some parsley for garnish after baking). On a floured surface roll out dough large enough to fit a baking sheet, then transfer, folding in the edges slightly to form a crust. Top with filling then transfer to oven and bake for 30-35 minutes until pastry is puffed and browning. If you don't have a baking stone, remove pastry to stovetop and cook over two burners on medium heat for an additional 6-8 minutes to crisp up the bottom (do not burn!). Remove from heat immediately, cut pieces using a pizza wheel or large knife.

Mussels, clams, and oysters are excellent sources of minerals, but can often be too "fishy" for many people, so baking them into a delicious pastry like this is a great way to include them in any diet.

Cheese and Peaches Tart

1 pastry dough (page 72) but with ½ cup added sugar
6-8 medium peaches, sliced somewhat thin
2 cups soft cheese (ricotta, cottage, blue, roquefort, etc)
½ cup sugar (brown sugar would be even better)
1 tsp cinnamon

Make a pastry dough (page 44), adding ½ cup of sugar to the dough when mixing. Preheat oven to 425°F (220°C), using a baking stone if you have one, and on a floured surface roll out dough to the size of a large baking sheet, transfer, then top with peaches, crumbled cheese, sugar, and dust with cinnamon. Fold edges of the tart over then bake in oven for about 30-35 minutes until the cheese barely starts to brown (mine went too long in the picture!). If you don't have a baking stone finish the tart on the stovetop burners on medium-low for an additional 6-7 minutes (do not burn!). Can be made into individual tarts if desired, otherwise cut with a pizza cutter and serve at room temperature.

The peaches provide plenty of carotene to prevent microbial production of hydrogen sulfide from the protein in the cheese and crust.

How to Salad

The point of salad is not for calorie cutting or dieting behaviors—but to provide a an indulgent way of eating healthy plant foods, and salad should be indulgent, interesting, and made of *high quality* ingredients. The most important point of a salad is the salt. The word 'salad' in fact means 'salted greens' and originates from ancient times, because people have been trying to eat healthy for millennia and is not something unique to today. Salads can take many forms, so be creative and indulgent, because eating healthy should be fun and satisfying.

Because commercial salad dressings often have harmful ingredients, it is wiser (and more economical) to make your own. Remember too that microbes require B12 to adhere to most plant foods, which normally comes from *Thaumarchaeota* archaea in turn dependent on vitamin D, which can be absent for many reasons, so using supplemental B12 mixed into salad dressing is an easy way to support gut microflora and digestion.

Steps
A salad is constructed of three basic stages: the vinaigrette or dressing, greens and other ingredients, and the salt. First, make the vinaigrette or dressing, then apply to the most abundant ingredient such as the lettuce, and toss— Waiting to toss the entire salad until the end will be difficult as the bowl fills, so tossing with the lettuce first makes this much easier. Add the remaining ingredients, then finish by sprinkling the salt over everything.

Dressing
Vinegar or lemon based dressings are most healthy because acids help promote digestion and neutralizes nitrates which promote opportunistic *Streptomyces* microbes which colonize the gut and impair commensal microbes and B vitamins. The addition of B12, selenium, or other required supplements to dressing is quite effective.

Ingredients
While lettuce is the easiest and most basic base for salad, a salad can be made of anything. But it is a myth that lettuce is not very nutritious because, if they have access to B12, gut microbes absolutely thrive on the high cellulose content of lettuce and produce from it an abundance of B vitamins, short chain fatty acids, amino acids, and combat opportunistic pathogens. Salads are in fact *very* filling precisely because of the microbial activity which results from such high cellulose consumption. Tough greens that taste bad raw, like kale, should *never* be eaten in salad because they contain *enzyme inhibitors* which can block digestion and require heat to inactivate. Some options for salad ingredients are: butter lettuce, romaine, red leaf, baby spinach, arugula (rocket), endive, microgreens, watercress, purslane, lambs lettuce, radicchio, mustard greens, dandelion greens, red cabbage, green cabbage, Napa cabbage, cucumber, radishes, carrot, peas, green beans, olives, tomatoes, red bell peppers, artichoke hearts, hearts of palm, beans, raisins, dried cranberries, crushed nuts, onions, green onions, chives, corn, hardboiled eggs, ham, chicken, sunflower seeds, pumpkin seeds, avocado, melon, tangerines, peaches, apples, berries, croutons (make some with olive oil and thyme from leftover bread), and cheese.

Basic Vinaigrette

¼ cup high quality olive oil, coconut oil, or high-oleic sunflower oil (not regular sunflower)

¼ cup vinegar or lemon juice

1 tsp ground black pepper

Whisk together the oil, vinegar, and pepper. Yes, it's that easy—the pepper helps increase emulsion so it comes together very rapidly. Try making variations including crushed garlic and sugar, mustard and honey, balsamic vinegar and crushed berries, etc.

Basic Salad

1 head romaine lettuce, quartered lengthwise then chopped into strips

1 large cucumber, halved longways, then sliced thin

3-4 tomatoes, cubed

1 carrot, peeled and finely shredded

1 cup good cheese, finely shredded

¼ cup almonds or hazelnuts, roughly crushed

1 can olives or hearts of palm, chopped

½ red cabbage, sliced thin

vinaigrette dressing

Peas and Cucumber

8 Persian cucumbers (or 3 large), sliced
1 pkg green peas (about 16 oz)
1 bunch fresh dill, chopped (about ¾ cup)
½ red onion, sliced
1 bunch purslane, chopped
1 vinaigrette (page 41) with 2 tsp added sugar
2 pinches salt

In a small pan over medium heat, cook the peas in a small amount of water for about 5 minutes until all the water evaporates (do not burn!). Remove from heat and allow to cool. Then, in a large bowl make the vinaigrette, add the cucumbers, salt and toss the dressing to fully coat, then stir in the peas, dill, red onion, and purslane. Especially since peas can be resistant to digestion, mixing B12 into the dressing can make this more nutritious.

Pea and cucumber are some of the best sources for molybdenum, a nutrient required for sulfur metabolism in our body. Skin malodor from sulfur foods (including protein) is a symptom of molybdenum deficiency, so use this salad or similar foods regularly, in the day, well preceding larger meals that contain dietary sulfur for best results. The purslane being high in oxalate will help prevent saponification of the fats.

Sautéed Yam with Salad

½ yam (true yam, not sweet potato)
2 tbsp coconut oil
1 tbsp butter
pinch salt
small salad (page 81)

Peel yam then cut into ½-inch slices. Melt oil and butter together in a large pan over medium heat. Add yam, sprinkle with salt, then cover and cook each side for about 8-10 minutes until they are nicely browned. While yam is cooking construct salad, and when yam is done serve hot next to or on top of salad. Also makes a great breakfast and can be served with fried or poached eggs.

True yam are even more delicious than sweet potatoes which often masquerade as yam, extremely healthy and full of indigestible carbohydrate that our microbiome love. This simple recipe will leave you feeling full and satiated for hours while helping to rehabilitate metabolic illnesses like diabetes and oral disease, especially if eating with a small dose of supplemental lithium to help evict gut parasites.

Brown Sugar, Basil, Lime Fruit Salad

raspberries, halved
strawberries, halved and de-leafed (after slicing in half the leaves can be pinched off easily)
nectarines, cubed
honeydew, cubed (optional)
½ cup good brown sugar
handful basil leaves, *julienned*
juice of 1-2 limes
pinch of salt

Chop fruit so they are generally bite-sized and add to a large bowl with the lime juice, basil, and pinch of salt and mix. Other fruits can be added or substituted, of course. Watermelon goes particularly well with this.

Fruit is probably the most important food that we can eat as human beings. Chock-full of important things like boron, potassium, and vitamin C, it's really hard to beat fruit's benefit to human health. Commercial fruit is often harvested underripe, however, which means its sugars are not easily digestible, and as much as possible fruit should be well-ripened. Growing your own or buying from local market gardeners is sometimes the only way to get ripe fruit. Most brown sugar at the grocery store is also white, refined sugar with added molasses. Make sure you get a high-quality, real brown sugar. Sucanat or muscovado are good examples.

Microgreens With Manchego

6 oz microgreens, chopped, preferably mixed varieties such as pea or sunflower as available
½ cup shaved manchego (use a vegetable peeler)
1 tbsp coconut oil, olive oil, or high-oleic sunflower oil
1 tbsp white vinegar or lemon juice
¼ tsp salt

In a medium or large bowl mix oil, vinegar, and salt. Whisk vigorously until it starts to thicken slightly. Add chopped microgreens and toss. Add shaved manchego and toss gently.

Microgreens are hands down some of the most healthy foods you can eat. They are so healthy, in fact, they are one of the few foods you can actually feel making you better after you eat them. The reason for this is because they have such compact nutrition both from the seed from which it germinated and the early burst of other nutrients created in the early stages of growth, and with reduced anti-nutrient factors from the sprouting process.

Nachos

20-25 nixtamalized corn tortillas, cut into 6ths
½ lb coconut oil
(or 1 bag high quality corn chips)
1 tsp salt + extra
1 can pinto beans
1 can black beans
1 can hominy
4 bay leaves

4 medium tomatoes, chopped
2 cups high quality cheese
1 cup tomatillo salsa (page 62) or other salsa
1 cup cilantro, chopped
Guacamole or avocado
Sour cream

First set the beans, hominy, bay leaves, and ¼ tsp salt to cook in a small pot over medium heat, then prepare salsa (page 62) if it's not already made. Next, preheat the oven to 350°F (175°C) and in a large pan or shallow pot over medium-high heat get the oil hot but not smoking (a test chip should sizzle robustly), then add the cut tortillas in several batches, turning occasionally to prevent burning until sizzling slows and chips begin to brown, remove with metal, slotted spoon, scatter on a large baking sheet, salting each time. When chips are done, top with cheese and tomatoes then place in oven for 10 minutes until cheese melts. Remove and top with beans (strain out liquid), onions, salsa, guacamole or avocado, cilantro, and sour cream as desired.

Nachos are not inherently healthy, but making them with high quality oil and lots of high polyphenol plant foods like tomatoes, onions, cilantro, and tomatillo salsa, and black beans is highly nutritious.

***Always exercise extreme caution when frying foods—hot oil can cause injury, so keep handles turned away from the front of the stove. Hot oil also catches fire quickly, if an oil fire occurs never dowse with water, immediately turn off heat and cover with a lid or extinguish with fire extinguisher.

Refried Beans for Tacos, Burritos, Dip

1 lb pinto beans, soaked at least 24 hours with ½ tsp baking soda (or 1-2 cans wet-packed pinto beans),
1 tsp salt
1 large onion, quartered
1 large onion, diced
1 head of garlic, peeled, whole cloves

1 tbsp ground cumin
1 tbsp oregano
½ cup coconut oil or lard
1 red bell pepper, seeded and minced
1-2 jalapeño peppers, seeded and minced

Preheat oven to 350°F (175°C). If using dried, soaked beans, add to a large pan or medium pot along with soaking water, the quartered onion, and the garlic cloves (smashed), the salt, and add enough water to cover beans about 1 inch. First bring to a simmer on the stove, then bake in the oven for about 3 hours until beans are very soft. Remove from oven and discard the onion (leave the garlic). In a large pan over medium heat sauté the jalapeño, red pepper, and the diced onion in the coconut oil for about 10 minutes until the onion is soft. Add the cumin and oregano and cook for another 5-6 minutes. Turn up the heat and add the beans along with their broth, stirring regularly until they begin to bubble. Using a potato masher mash the beans until they are smooth. Serve in grilled tortillas topped with cheese and toppings like fresh chopped onion, cilantro, red cabbage, lime, avocado, diced tomatoes, etc., or beans can be used in burritos, or topped with cotija cheese and cilantro and dipped with freshly made corn chips.

Legumes such as beans are very high in potassium and good sources of molybdenum and lysine, but they can be very hard to digest and must be prepared properly. Beans harden when exposed to acid, so the inclusion of baking soda in the soaking liquid helps soften beans better. During iodine deficiency legumes can also cause problems like hair loss, due to their phytoestrogens, but which is a problem of iodine deficiency, not legumes, just account for such factors.

Kabocha Tomatillo Soft Tacos

1 kabocha squash, halved and seeded
1 tbsp coconut oil
1 lb tomatillos, hulled and washed
5-6 cloves garlic, peeled and chopped
1 tsp salt
1 tsp ground cumin
1 tsp oregano
½ tsp cayenne powder

8-10 soft corn tortillas
Optional toppings:
cheese, shredded or crumbled
½ onion, diced
cilantro
avocado
Mexican crema or sour cream
hot sauce and salsa

Preheat oven to 400°F (200°C). Place kabocha cut side down on a large baking sheet in oven to cook for 20 minutes to soften up the skin. While the squash cooks, heat a large pan over medium-high and grill the tortillas, about 30 seconds on each side. Remove squash from oven, remove skin, and cut into cubes. In the large pan over medium-high heat add the coconut oil and tomatillos whole. They should start to scorch, then toss or turn every 5 minutes until many sides are scorched. Add the cubed squash, garlic, cumin, oregano, cayenne, and salt, then cover and allow to cook until the tomatillos break open and come to a simmer. Season to taste then remove from heat and serve in tortillas topped with things like cheese, onion, and cilantro, crema, or other toppings as desired.

Kabocha also makes a great taco if it is properly accompanied by tart flavors and earthy spices, and the use of tomatillo adds more interest, bulk, and nutrition. The high carotene of the kabocha naturally helps protect the protein and sulfur from microbial hydrogen sulfide producers.

Dinners

Roast Winter Squash

1 winter squash per 2 people (kombucha, acorn, butternut, honeynut, etc.)

¼ tsp salt

1 tbsp butter

Preheat oven to 400°F (200°C). Using a large knife carefully cut squash into halves, removing seeds. Place onto a baking tray cut side down and cook for 1 hour until the squash is soft when pierced with a knife. Remove from oven, slice into servings, and top with salt and butter.

Sautéed Greens

1 bunch cruciferous or other greens (collards, kale, chard, spinach, Brussels sprouts, etc.)

¼ tsp salt

4 tbsp butter and 4 tbsp coconut oil

Chop greens loosely, then in a large pan over medium-high heat melt the butter, add greens and salt then cover, stirring every minute to prevent burning, until greens are well cooked and even start to char slightly. *Do not overcook!* When starting to char remove and serve.

Sautéed Green Beans

1 lb fresh green beans

¼ tsp salt

4 tbsp butter and 4 tbsp coconut oil

Over medium heat melt the butter and coconut oil in a large pan. Remove hard stems from beans, add to pan, sprinkle with salt, and cover, cooking for a good 10-15 minutes, stirring occasionally, until the beans are very slightly scorched. Make sure to drain oil from pan onto beans when serving.

Mashed Yam

1 large yam (not sweet potato…real yam), peeled and cubed large

1 tsp ground black pepper

1 tsp salt

4 tbsp butter

½ cup milk

Boil yam cubes for 18-20 minutes until soft. Drain water then mash yam with remaining ingredients.

Every meal needn't be a production. Just cook some vegetables and eat them with butter, salt, and pepper, or serve these as sides at a larger meal.

Pan Roasted Potatoes

3-4 pounds potatoes, peeled and cubed
¼ cup olive oil
1 head garlic, peeled and minced
1 tbsp thyme
2 tsp ground black pepper
2 tsp salt
½ cup high quality, hard cheese (like parmesan or romano)

Preheat oven to 400°F (200°C). In a large pan or skillet, add the potatoes then fill pan with water halfway up the potatoes and no more, then set over high heat and bring to a simmer. While the water is heating up, add the olive oil, garlic, thyme, pepper, salt, and cheese onto the potatoes and stir to distribute evenly. After it comes to a simmer transfer pan to the oven and bake for 70-90 minutes, turning the potatoes halfway through, until the water is gone and the potatoes are lightly browned.

Potatoes are excellent sources of potassium, carbs, vitamin C, and oxalate, the latter of which helps protect the fats in butter and olive oil from saponification in the gut.

Roast Chicken or Turkey

1 whole chicken or turkey (or a selection of parts)
1-2 tsp salt, depending on size
1-2 tbsp coconut oil or olive oil, depending on size
cooking string (optional)

2 hours before cooking remove bird from the refrigerator and allow it to come to room temperature. Rinse the bird and pat dry with some paper towels, then truss the carcass with the string (look online to see how to do this if you don't already know), place in a large dutch oven or roasting pan and cover with the oil and salt (make sure you have removed the giblets from the inside if they are included). Most people cook poultry breast up, which looks fancy but it's actually better to flip the bird breast down, so the normally dry breast meat will be juicier (bird can be turned breast up the last ¼ cooking time if desired). Move bird to the oven, set the temperature to 350°F (180°C), and cook about 80 minutes for a chicken or 3 hours for a turkey, depending on size, until the bird is browned and the meat registers 160°F (71°C) by a meat thermometer. When done remove from oven and allow to rest ten minutes before carving. After eating, save carcass and giblets for stock (page 114) or gravy.

NEVER put poultry into a preheated oven or already boiling water—Always bring poultry to room temperature then turn on the oven only after the meat is inside (same with boiling). Also, never brine poultry—it just absorbs the water and becomes flavorless and soggy. Just use salt directly on the bird.

Pasta

2 cups flour (spelt, einkorn, or kamut)
3 large eggs (or 4 medium)
2-3 tbsp salt (for the water)

In a large bowl add the flour, make a well in the center, then crack eggs into the well. Using a fork, scramble the eggs till smooth then begin drawing the flour into the eggs at a moderate pace, mixing thoroughly each time. Once the dough comes together turn onto the counter and continue to mix by hand-kneading until all the flour is incorporated and dough is smooth (about 5-8 minutes). The dough should be dry enough to preventing sticking to itself when cutting pasta but not so dry that it becomes impossible to roll. Form into a ball, cover, and allow to rest for at least 10 minutes.

While the dough is resting, fill a very large pot halfway with water and 2-3 tbsp of salt and bring to a boil while preparing the pasta sauce from a desired recipe. Most pasta sauces incorporate some of pasta water, so salting the water adds seasoning to both the pasta and sauce while flour leached from cooking helps sauce thicken, so boiling the pasta concurrently to constructing the sauce is a vital part of making pasta.

After the sauce is cooking, generously flour the countertop and, using a roller, roll dough into a large rectangle until the pasta is sufficiently thin (if your countertop is small you can cut the dough in two and do this twice). At all times dough should easily slip around the counter under the pin, if this does not occur the dough is too wet and more flour should be added under and over the dough to prevent sticking. When the dough is fully rolled cover generously with a light layer of flour, spreading with hands, then take the long side of the rectangle and fold onto itself, about 3 inches. Add more flour on top of each fold and repeat until all the dough is folded. Use a large knife to cut into pasta at the desired width. Then lift and separate all the pasta—if it's dry enough this should occur simply from tossing, otherwise unroll each strip manually by hand. Pasta can sit, uncovered, until water is boiling and sauce is ready, then transfer pasta to water, stirring gently to prevent sticking, until pasta floats at the surface (about 1-2 minutes). Transfer pasta to sauce with one or two ladles of pasta water as directed in sauce recipe. Toss pasta and sauce together, cooking for several minutes until the sauce thickens.

Many pasta recipes are formulated incorrectly—the only ingredients that should generally go into pasta dough are flour and eggs or water. Salt causes gluten proteins in flour to stiffen, and oil makes pasta more prone to breaking, and these ingredients should be added in the cooking water and sauce, not to the pasta dough itself. This recipe is also for 2-4 people (or leftovers), so adjust accordingly as needed.

Pasta and Mushrooms

pasta dough as prepared on page 104
3 tbsp salt
6 tbsp butter
2-3 shallots, peeled and minced
2-3 packages of brown button mushrooms, minced
½ tsp salt
1 tsp ground black pepper
½ cup good hard cheese (parmesan, manchego, etc.), shredded
2 tbsp fresh parsley, minced (for garnish)
1 cup white wine (optional)

First make pasta dough, then set aside. Fill a large pot halfway with water, add the 3 tbsp salt, cover and set to boil. While water is heating sauté shallots, mushrooms, salt, and pepper in the butter in a large pan over medium heat until the mushrooms are soft and shrunk, about 10 minutes. When the sauce is almost done cut and boil the pasta. After pasta floats to the surface, ladle 1 scoop of pasta water into the mushrooms then transfer pasta from water to the mushrooms. Using two large utensils, toss gently until the sauce thickens and is no longer watery. Remove from heat and add cheese, tossing until it melts. When serving top with more shredded cheese, fresh minced parsley, and a little more ground black pepper as desired.

*mushrooms are very healthy, and having them in a pasta is just pure comfort food. If you have some white wine you can add ½ cup to the sauce for a more complex flavor. Making sure to mince the mushrooms helps release more of their delicate flavor, but they can also be sliced instead of minced.

Pasta with Tomatoes and Garlic

pasta as prepared on page 104
3 tbsp salt
1 whole head of garlic, peeled
1 tbsp olive oil
2 tbsp butter
2 tsp ground black pepper

Pinch salt
3-4 pounds of high quality tomatoes, cut into 1 inch wide slices or cubes
2 tsp thyme
1 ladle hot pasta water
2 cups high quality cheese, shredded (such as parmesan, manchego)

First make pasta dough and roll out into a large rectangle on a floured surface. Then, fill a large pot halfway with water, add 3 tbsp of salt, cover and set to boil. While water is heating up, add the butter and olive oil to a large pan over medium heat and sauté the garlic with the pepper and pinch of salt for five minutes, stirring slowly to avoid browning. Then, and add the tomatoes and thyme, raise the heat to medium-high and cook for about 15 minutes until the juices begin to thicken, stirring occasionally to prevent burning. While the sauce cooks, roll and cut pasta. When the sauce thickens boil the pasta then transfer to sauce along with 1 ladle (about ¾ cup) of the pasta water. Using two large utensils, slowly toss pasta as it cooks until the sauce thickens again (about 5 minutes). Remove from heat, stir in cheese and allow to melt before serving. Garnish with extra cheese and ground pepper, if desired.

this tomato pasta is ideal for supplying dietary sulfur in the garlic, cheese, and pasta, since the high carotene of the tomatoes blocks microbial hydrogen sulfide production, specifically the lycopene in tomatoes which is not fully absorbed, meaning more of it stays in the gut to inhibit harmful microbes. Alternatively this can be made with canned tomatoes when fresh ones are not available.

Spinach Pasta

2 cups frozen spinach (1 cup cooked)
2 cups flour + 1 cup
2 eggs
3 tbsp salt
½ cup butter

1 head garlic, peeled and smashed
1-2 cups high quality cheese, shredded
½ tsp ground black pepper

First cook the spinach in a large, shallow pan (use a small amount of coconut oil to prevent sticking) over medium heat until the spinach is as dry as possible, without browning. When spinach is done, set aside to cool completely. Fill a large pot ½ way with water, add the salt, then set over high heat to boil. Mince spinach well then add to a small bowl with the eggs and mix until fully combined. In a large bowl add the flour then in the center make a well and the eggs and spinach. Using a fork, slowly draw in the flour to the eggs until most of the flour is incorporated, turn onto a floured countertop and knead, mixing and kneading in more flour until the dough is smooth and no longer wet (very important). Roll dough on a floured surface, fold and cut pasta. Then in the pan add the butter and garlic and cook over low heat for about 10 minutes until garlic is well softened and only barely browned, boil pasta then transfer to pan with 1 ladle of pasta water, using two large utensils to stir gently until sauce thickens. Remove from heat, fold in cheese, and top with pepper before serving.

*the point of spinach pasta is the pasta itself, so sauces should not be heavy or obscure it too much. Because spinach has silicon, oxalate, and vitamin K, this is an excellent dish to support a variety of health needs such as calcium metabolism, sulfation, and cholesterol support. The large chunks of soft garlic are especially delicious.

Curried Cauliflower

1/4 cup coconut oil
7-9 bay leaves
2 yellow onions, chopped large
5-6 carrots, chopped large
1 head garlic, smashed but whole cloves
2 tsp salt
2 tsp ground black pepper
1-2 large cauliflower, cubed large
4 red bell peppers, seeded and chopped large

1 lb high quality tomatoes, chopped large
2 cups real coconut cream or creamed coconut
2 inch of ginger root, peeled and diced
1 cup peanuts with skins (optional)
¼ cup curry powder
1 cup fresh parsley, chopped
Brown rice, soaked overnight (12-24 hours) or white rice, unsoaked

First bring rice to a boil in its soaking water (1 inch of water on top of rice), then reduce heat to low, cover, and cook until water is absorbed and evaporated, about 30 minutes. While the rice is cooking, sauté the bay leaves, onion, carrots, garlic, salt, and pepper in the coconut oil in a very large pot over medium-high heat (to slightly scorch vegetables) until the onion begins to turn translucent (about 10-12 minutes). Add tomatoes, cauliflower, and red bell pepper and cook for another five minutes, then add the coconut cream, ginger, peanuts, and curry powder and mix well, reduce heat to medium-low and cover, continue to cook for another 15-20 minutes until cauliflower is soft but not overcooked. Remove from heat and stir in the parsley. Serve over rice (remove bay leaves while serving).

*something about curried cauliflower makes it addicting, and this dish is high in nutrition, carotene, tannins, and cinnamic acids (mostly from the turmeric in curry powder). I also like making this dish because there is less chopping and it comes together much faster than other dishes.

Stock

8-10 carrots, chopped
1 bunch celery, chopped
2-3 onions, chopped (*do not discard peel*)
2 tbsp salt
1 tsp whole black peppercorns
Extra vegetable parts as desired, such as leek tops, a parsnip, or seeded chiles

For meat stocks, add one type of meat as desired:
4-6 chicken parts or a whole carcass, with skin and bones
4-5 beef bone pieces
4-5 pork bones or leftovers
fish skin, shrimp shells, clam packing water, etc.

Fill a very large pot with about 2 gallons of water (about ¾ the way on most large pots is just fine, my pot is so large I only fill it ½ way with water). Add all the ingredients, cover, and bring to a boil, then reduce to a low simmer and boil for about 4 hours. When the stock is done, first lift out most of the ingredients using a slotted spoon and strainer or colander and discard. After most ingredients are removed, drain the stock into a large bowl through a strainer or colander, then use stock as desired. Freeze any leftovers in food-safe, freezer-safe containers.

*Quality of ingredients matter a great deal for delicious stock. Any extra vegetable parts can be used (save scraps from other meals) but don't use strongly flavored vegetables like brassicas unless the stock is being used in a dish that includes those.

*tannins strengthen plant cell walls which prevents flavor release, so **do not** *use bay leaves when making stock, but add to recipes directly instead.*

*If you have problems with migraines, cancer, or gut health, immerse high nitrate vegetables like celery or other leafy greens in water for a few minutes **before** *using in stock (nitrate is water soluble) then discard that water.*

*Many soup ingredients like beans, garlic, peas, and other vegetables contain an abundance of indigestible carbohydrate like cellulose which human digestion is not capable of breaking down without healthy gut microbes which require vitamin B12 (cobalamin), and it can be added to stock after cooking in order to improve digestibility. Soup is a good vehicle for other fortification too, such as a single drop of iodine added to the whole batch for thyroid health (never use excess as that can oppositely suppress gut microbes), or selenium to promote cholesterol production.

Corn, Cabbage, and Potato

4 tbsp butter
4 cloves garlic, peeled and crushed
3 large dried Anaheim or guajillo chiles, seeded
4 quarts stock
1-2 lbs wet-pack nixtamalized corn (hominy)
2 cans cannellini beans
1 can red kidney beans
2 lbs potatoes, peeled and cubed
1 head red cabbage (or 2 small), chopped thin
2 tbsp salt
1 tbsp ground black pepper

In a large pot over medium heat melt the butter and sauté the garlic and chiles for about 5 minutes. Add the stock and bring to a boil, then add the corn and cook, covered, for about 30 minutes to ensure the grains are soft. Add the beans, potatoes, cabbage, celery, salt, and pepper. Bring back to a simmer then cover and cook for and additional 30 minutes, then remove the chiles (Anaheim chiles are not very hot but guajillo may not be suitable for those sensitive to spice and any mild chiles will work great and adds more complex and savory flavor—be sure to remove the seeds, which contain the most heat and cause rapid evacuation due to their high serotonin).

Didn't expect a purple soup? Purple varieties of corn, potatoes, and cabbage contain pigments called anthocyanin which are some of the healthiest plant compounds we can consume and directly benefit the cardiovascular system, hair growth, and libido. On its own cabbage is not very tasty, so the addition of corn and chiles add sweetness and depth. For darker soup try to get all purple varieties of ingredients, but even one will impart a lovely, deep hue that is as nutritional as it is interesting.

Chicken Soup

2 tbsp butter
10 medium carrots
4 garlic cloves
6-8 bay leaves
3-4 quarts chicken stock (make your own on page 114)
1 tbsp salt (only add if broth is not already salted)
2 tsp ground black pepper
Egg pasta dough (page 104) or premade, wide pasta
2-3 cups cooked chicken
1 cup peas

If making pasta by hand (it only takes 10 minutes!) make pasta dough first and set aside. In a large soup pot over medium-high heat sauté the carrots, garlic, and bay leaves in the butter for about 8 minutes, then add the stock and salt (only if the broth is *not* already salted, add to taste) and pepper, bring to a low simmer and allow the carrots to cook for an additional 10-12 minutes until they are soft but not overcooked. While the soup is cooking, roll the pasta out in one large, rectangular sheet and quite thin. Fold and cut as directed on page 104 in ¾ inch wide strips. Unfold pasta, and when the carrots are done add the chicken and peas to the pot, cook for 5 minutes, then add pasta and cook only another 2 minutes, stirring gently to prevent sticking. Remove immediately from heat and allow to rest/cool for about 5-10 minutes (it's really hot!). Garish with chopped parsley if desired for some added vitamin K.

Chicken soup is such a fundamental meal for healing, but which has almost nothing to do with chicken and is instead a function of its high chloride content that supports the immune reaction. Adding plenty of bay leaves for more tannin can further support immune function by helping to arrest growth of gut microbes. The pasta can always be swapped with rice or potatoes for other great variation.

Garlic Kabocha Soup

2 kabocha squash (or other winter squash or pumpkin), halved and seeded
3 tbsp butter
1 large onion, chopped
2 entire heads of garlic, peeled and chopped
5-6 bay leaves
4-5 quarts stock or broth (vegetable or chicken, page 45)
1 tsp salt
2 tsp ground black pepper

Set the oven to 400°F (200°C). Cut squash in half, seed, and place cut side down onto a baking sheet and into oven. Roast for about 70-80 minutes until squash skin is browned and flesh is softened (there will be juices blackening on the pan as well). Remove squash and allow to cool completely, then remove skin and discard. In a large soup pot over medium heat add the butter, onions, garlic, bay leaves, salt, and pepper and sauté for 10 minutes until onions are soft and translucent (do not brown). Transfer to a large bowl, remove bay leaves, then in a blender, in batches, add stock, squash, and onions and blend smooth. Return everything to soup pot, bring to a boil and cook for about 5-6 minutes, stirring occasionally. Serve with crusty bread.

Kabocha is a delicious squash that has more flavor and texture than other varieties, and is an excellent source of carotene which helps protect the high amount of sulfur in so much garlic from hydrogen sulfide producing microbes, but other winter varieties of squash can be used. Optionally, add well-cooked cannellini beans for more protein and a thicker soup.

Split Pea Soup

1 lb dried split peas
2 tbsp olive oil
6 cloves garlic, peeled and diced
1 onion, minced
5-6 bay leaves
1 quart water
2 tsp salt
1 tsp ground black pepper

The night before cooking, add dried peas to a bowl and cover with 1 inch of water, allow to soak overnight. The next day in a medium or large pot over medium heat add the olive oil, onion, and garlic and sauté until the onion becomes very translucent and soft. Add the soaked peas, including their soaking water, an additional 1 quart of water, and the salt and pepper. Cover and cook for 1 hour or until the peas start to fall apart and are no longer firm. Serve with really crusty bread.

Peas are an especially good source of molybdenum and lysine, but peas are also high in fiber and during the wintertime or other sunlight deficiency (or that of vitamin D) they can result in substantial gas production by methanogenic microbes in the gut. If that is the case, make sure to add a dose of B12 to the soup for better digestion and reduced gas production.

This recipe makes an obscene amount, so halve it if you don't have a large pot or many mouths to feed

Minestrone

1 package dried, small pasta like ditalini, cavatelli, shells, or macaroni, or make your own (optional)
2 large onions, minced
1 head garlic, peeled and chopped
8-10 medium carrots, peeled and chopped
4 tbsp olive oil
10 bay leaves
2 tsp salt
1 tsp ground black pepper
2 lbs crushed tomatoes (fresh or canned)
4 quarts water
2 lbs green beans, de-stemmed and chopped
1 can red kidney beans
1 can white beans (great northern, cannellini, etc.)
4 stalks celery, chopped ¼ inch thick
1 lb green peas
1 bunch asparagus (optional), chopped
¼ cup fresh parsley, minced

In a very large soup pot over medium heat sauté the onion, carrots, garlic, salt, pepper, and bay leaves in the olive oil until the onions are translucent, about 10 minutes. Then add the tomatoes, water, celery, and all the beans and bring to a simmer, covered, for about thirty minutes, stirring occasionally to prevent burning. If making pasta do so while the soup cooks. After it's done, add the pasta, peas, and asparagus to the soup and bring back to a simmer until the pasta is cooked. Remove from heat immediately and remove bay leaves.

Minestrone simply means 'thick vegetable soup' in Italian, and is the Italian answer to chicken soup in terms of a dish given to those who are sick and need healing. Minestrone is indeed one of the most comforting dishes and though it takes a little effort to put together it can be made in a large batch with plenty of leftovers. Any vegetables can be used in minestrone, but in my opinion the point of it is an indulgent vehicle for green beans, which are high in silicon and thus help to heal cancer and normalize hormones. No need to use stock for this soup—there's already so much flavor!

White Bean and Mushroom

4 tbsp butter
4-6 leeks, chopped and washed
4-6 cloves of garlic, peeled and chopped
4 packages (2 lbs) brown mushrooms, sliced
5-6 bay leaves
2 tsp salt
1 tsp ground black pepper

¼ cup flour
4 quarts vegetable stock
6 cans (16 oz) cannellini beans
1 bunch watercress, minced
½ cup half and half
Salt and pepper to taste

In a large pot over medium-heat sauté leeks in the butter until they begin to soften (about 5-6 minutes), add the mushrooms, garlic, bay leaves, salt, and pepper and continue cooking until the mushrooms have shed some water and shrunk a little. Sprinkle evenly with flour, mix, and continue cooking for another 3-4 minutes. Add the stock and beans, bring to a simmer then cover and lower heat to low and cook for about 30 minutes until the beans soften. Add the watercress, remove from heat and use a potato masher to break up some of the beans to thicken the soup (remove bay leaves too). Stir in the half and half and season to taste.

this mushroom soup is lighter and more flavorful than typical cream of mushroom, because the white beans fall apart during cooking and help thicken the soup instead of relying entirely on cream. The use of beans also makes it far more nutritious, but make sure if it's wintertime to add some B12 to the soup to help the microbiome break down the high amount of indigestible carbohydrate, otherwise this recipe will result in a lot of gas. Dried cannellinis could be soaked and cooked prior to making the soup and used instead of canned, but I can't get them to turn out as soft as canned.

Hearty Cream and Vegetable

1/2 stick of butter (4-5 tbsp)
1 large onion, diced.
6-7 bay leaves
3 cloves of garlic, smashed.
1 tsp salt
5 or 6 carrots, peeled + chopped
4 or 5 small yellow squash (2-3 large), 3/4 inch slices
1/2 head of cauliflower broken into pieces
3-4 small or 1-2 large yellow potatoes, peeled and chopped

1 green bell pepper, seeded and sliced
1 red bell pepper, seeded and sliced
2 cups cherry tomatoes, halved
1 tsp paprika or cajun seasoning
1/2 tsp cayenne pepper
2 quarts vegetable broth
1 pint heavy cream
1 cup parsley, chopped

In a large soup pot melt butter, add diced onion, garlic, and salt, sauté on high until just turning yellow. Add carrot, paprika, and cayenne and continue sauté for another five minutes until just before onions brown. Add remaining vegetables (except parsley) and broth. Bring to boil then cover and simmer on medium-low heat for about 40 minutes until all vegetables turn soft, stirring occasionally, tasting for flavor toward the end and adding more salt if needed. When squash and cauliflower fall apart it's done. Remove from heat, remove bay leaves, then mash some vegetables to thicken slightly but not all, to retain chunkiness. Add parsley and cream, stir together and serve, garnish with a few leaves of parsley.

This stew is a classic comfort dish of cream and vegetables sweetened by carrots and spiced enough to offset and enliven the cream. The carotene of the carrots helps protect the sulfur from reduction by hydrogen sulfide producers while the oxalate in potatoes and parsley helps prevent saponification of the fats.

Garden Greens

6 tbsp butter
2 tbsp olive oil
1 large onion, minced
1 head garlic, chopped
6-8 bay leaves
2 tsp salt
1 tsp ground black pepper
4-5 quarts stock

2 lbs cannellini beans (wet-pack or pre-cooked)
1 head celery, chopped
1 lb green beans, chopped
3 bunches fresh adult spinach, whole
1 bunch collard greens, chopped
1 head Napa cabbage, chopped thin
3 bunches watercress, chopped
1 pkg frozen green peas

Before doing anything, immerse all the leafy greens in water and let them sit for 5 minutes. This will help remove a lot of their nitrate content, then drain and discard water. Next, in a large pot over medium heat sauté the onion, garlic, bay leaves, salt, and pepper in the butter and olive oil until the onions become translucent, careful not to brown the garlic. Sprinkle with flour, mix, and continue cooking for another 2-3 minutes. Add the spinach, collards, cabbage, stock, and beans then bring to a boil, reduce heat and cook for about 10 minutes until the cabbage is soft but not overcooked. Add the watercress and green peas and cook for another 5 minutes. Remove from heat, discard bay leaves and serve.

*this soup is an easy way to get plenty of vitamin K and thiocyanate. Good any time greens are available, but because leafy greens are often high in nitrates they can cause some problems if care is not taken to first remove some. Nitrate is highly water soluble, so immersing in water is and then discarding the water is useful. Nitrate is also neutralized by acid, so the addition of vitamin C, citric acid, or vinegar can also help.

Black Bean and Red Pepper Stew

2 lbs dried black beans
5-6 large red bell peppers, seeded and sliced longways
1 large yellow onion (or two medium), minced
1 head garlic, smashed
5-6 bay leaves
8 tbsp butter

2 tsp salt
2 cans (28 oz each) crushed tomatoes
2-3 tbsp fresh oregano (dried is fine)
2 quarts stock (prepare with some chiles)
¼ cup parsley, diced (optional garnish)

beef can be added to this recipe if desired, and is very good. Sear a roast then braise with the beans for 3-4 hours until it falls apart and beans are fully cooked.

A day or two before making stew, cover beans with 1 inch of water in a large bowl and soak at least 24 hours (do *not* change water during soaking). When making the stock for this soup, add California chiles (remove seeds) for a more savory broth. Bake beans in a large, oven-safe dish for about 3 hours at 325° F (160) until they are soft but not overcooked. When beans are done, sauté the onion, garlic, and bay leaves in the butter and salt in a large pot over medium heat until they are soft but not browned. Then add the beans and their baking liquid, the peppers, oregano, tomatoes, and broth, bring to a low boil and cook for 45 minutes until the peppers are soft.

bell peppers are some of the most potent dietary sources of vitamin C, but they also contain both carotene and anthocyanins, and this is an especially hearty and comforting soup. Add a little B12 (after cooking, not during), even if you're getting plenty of sunshine, for easier digestion of the beans.

Cream of Broccoli

4 tbsp butter
4 tbsp coconut oil
1 yellow onion, minced
1 head garlic, crushed and chopped
7-8 bay leaves
1 tbsp salt

4-5 quarts stock
2 lbs yellow potatoes, cubed small
2 cans cannellini beans
6-7 heads of broccoli, chopped small
2-3 heads huauzontle (optional)
1 cup heavy cream

In a large soup pot sauté the onion, garlic, and bay leaves in the butter and salt over medium heat until the onions are very soft and translucent but not browned. Add the stock, potatoes, and beans and their juices. Bring to a simmer, cover, and cook for 70-80 minutes until the beans and potatoes begin to fall apart. Add the broccoli and huauzontle and cook for another 20 minutes until soft. Use a potato masher to break up all the potato and beans, then remove from heat and stir in the cream (for a smoother soup run potatoes and beans through a blender *before* adding broccoli).

*Cream soups are often thickened with starch and cream, but using whole vegetables like potatoes or cannellini beans not only thickens effectively but improves flavor and nutrition. Cream of broccoli is an excellent source of vitamin K and thiocyanate. Huauzontle is a bit like broccoli but with a high amount of oxalates which protect the fat in this cream soup from saponification by opportunistic microbes (if you can't find huauzontle drink tea with the meal or use another oxalate source).

Bread and Onion Soup

6 large, yellow onions, sliced
8 tbsp (1/2 cup) butter
1 tbsp salt
1 head garlic, peeled and chopped
6-7 bay leaves
22 tsp ground black pepper
4-5 quarts stock
2 cups bread, cubed large
2 cups good cheese, shredded

First, cube the bread then set aside, uncovered, to dry (several hours beforehand is ideal). Then in a large pot over medium heat sauté the onions in butter and salt until they start to turn brown and caramelize. This takes up to an hour, so they can be covered and left to cook, stirring occasionally to prevent burning, stirring more frequently as they start to darken, even adding a little water if they dry out. When the onions are quite browned add the garlic, bay leaves, and pepper and stir sufficiently often to prevent garlic from burning, another 10 minutes. When the onions are nicely browned and extremely soft, add the stock, bring to a simmer, reduce heat to low, cover, and let cook for another 30 minutes. Remove from heat, serve soup into bowls (only about ¾ full) then add the bread cubes and cheese on top, letting the cheese melt from the heat of the soup.

This recipe is an excellent way to get a lot of dietary sulfur required for sulfation of fats, hormones, and detox pathways, but it doesn't contain many protective nutrients and will required carrots or other high-carotene food alongside it to suppress hydrogen sulfide producers.

Tomato Soup

1 large, yellow onion, minced
1 head garlic, peeled and chopped
8 tbsp (1/2 cup) butter
6-7 bay leaves
1 tbsp salt
1 tsp ground black pepper

½ cup flour
4 quarts stock
2 cans cannellini beans
2 large cans crushed tomatoes (or use several pounds fresh tomatoes, blanch to remove skins)

In a large pot over medium heat, sauté the onions, garlic, and bay leaves in butter with the salt and pepper until the onions are very soft and beginning to brown. Stir in the flour and cook for an additional 5 minutes (to remove the raw flour taste), then add the stock, beans, and tomatoes, stir well and bring to a simmer then cover and let cook for a full hour or until the beans become soft. After an hour, use a strainer or slotted spoon to remove bay leaves, then transfer solids (beans, onions, etc.) and a little soup to a blender to blend smooth (or use an immersion blender), then return to the soup. Serve with lots of crusty, fresh bread or grilled cheese sandwiches.

Tomato soup being very high in carotene is an excellent vehicle for high sulfur foods like onions and garlic since the carotene naturally protects against microbial hydrogen sulfide producers. Served with grilled cheese is an excellent food for kids or adults who want to revisit their childhood while also eating healthy. The addition of canelinis makes the soup more hearty but might require B12 to digest properly during winter.

Pork with Purslane and Tomatillos

2-3 lbs pork
2 tsp salt
2 tbsp coconut oil
2 medium onions, diced
1 head garlic, peeled and crushed
2-3 lbs tomatillos, de-husked

1 lb purslane
4-6 corn tortillas per person, grilled
2 tbsp parsley or cilantro, diced
1-2 limes, juiced

In a large pot over medium-high heat place the coconut oil and salt, brown the pork in the oil, searing each side for about 5 minutes. Reserve ½ cup of minced onions for garnish, then reduce heat to medium-low and add the onions, garlic, and tomatillos then cover and allow to cook for 2 ½ to 3 hours until pork falls apart, stirring occasionally to prevent burning (more important toward the end). The tomatillos will slowly fall apart during cooking but if it starts to dry out at the end add a little water (about ½ cup at a time) to prevent burning. While the pork cooks grill the tortillas in a large, dry pan over high heat, cooking each side no more than 30 seconds (it's done when it starts bubbling on the top side). When the pork falls apart, add the purslane and while the purslane cooks use a large utensil to break apart the pork. Remove from heat, squeeze limes into pork, and serve with tortillas, onions, and cilantro. Goes well with beans, beans and rice, or yuca dish.

Purslane is a very healthy vegetable high in oxalate, which helps to protect the gut (and food) from pathogens by binding to calcium, and dietary calcium oxalate is mostly metabolized into acetic acid by commensal gut microbes. Tomatillos are delicious and bathe the pork and purslane in a tangy richness.

Savory Bread Pudding

3-4 cups leftover bread, cubed, dried
2 cups chicken, cooked, cubed
2-3 cups chicken broth (depending on amount of bread)
4 large eggs
1/2 cup cream
4 oz goat cheese broken into large crumbles
1/2 tsp sea salt

Cut leftover bread into 3/4 inch cubes and allow to dry out for a few hours. Preheat oven to 350° F (177° C). Fry chicken until almost done but not fully cooked, remove from heat and cube. In a large bowl add eggs, cream, broth, and salt, then beat until combined. Add bread, chicken, and goat cheese crumbles to liquid and stir gently until all is coated and soaked. Turn out mixture into a large soufflé or casserole dish and bake for about 40 minutes until top is browned and crispy.

Bread pudding is not always sweet! In fact, I much prefer the savory type such as this recipe. Bread with fats and tasty meats and seasonings all in one dish—there's nothing more indulgent, but this dish entirely lacks protective phytonutrients and is just here because it's fucking delicious, and as such should be accompanied by carotene and oxalates if suffering from any kind of metabolic disease (some tea with the meal would be sufficient).

Broccoli Risotto

1 package (1 lb) arborio rice (pearl rice works too)
2 quarts stock
4 tbsp butter
2 tbsp olive oil
5 cloves garlic
4 crowns of broccoli, chopped small (discard stems)

1-2 stems huauzontle (optional)
1 tsp salt
1 tsp ground black pepper
1 cup high quality cheese, shredded (parmesan, aged cheddar, etc.)
juice of ½ lemon

Before making risotto bring the stock to a simmer in a separate pot. Then add the butter, olive oil, garlic, and pepper to a large pan over medium heat (a large pot can work too) followed by the rice. Allow the rice and garlic to toast for about 5 minutes, stirring regularly to prevent garlic from browning. Then add the stock several ladles at a time, stirring until the rice begins to absorb the stock and adding more as needed to prevent it from drying out. After about 6-7 ladles of stock add the broccoli (and huauzontle if you have it) and continue adding stock until the rice is slow to take up liquid and grains are al dente (cooked but not mushy). You will likely not use all the stock. Remove from heat and stir in the salt, cheese, and lemon juice until the cheese is fully melted and combined. Serve with good bread and wine or as a side for a larger meal (white wine can also be added to the recipe if desired).

Risotto is really comforting and a great medium by which to add healthy food items like vitamin K rich broccoli. This dish is surprisingly flavorful and indulgent, while the vitamin K in the broccoli helps us properly metabolize the calcium content in the cheese. The huauzontle is there for its oxalates to help prevent fat saponification in the gut. If you don't have access to that take tea with this meal to do the same since tea is high in oxalate.

Mushroom Risotto

4 tbsp butter
1 onion, finely diced or grated
1 tsp ground black pepper
1 tsp salt
4 cloves garlic, minced
2 packages brown mushrooms, sliced

1 tsp dried thyme
1 package (1 lb) arborio rice (pearl rice works too)
2 quarts high quality stock or broth
1 cup high quality cheese (parmesan, manchego, etc.)

Before making risotto bring stock to a simmer in a medium pot. Then in a large pan over medium heat add the butter, onions, salt, and pepper and cook for about 8 minutes until the onions are soft but without color. Add the mushrooms, garlic, and thyme, cook while stirring regularly until the mushrooms shrink and give off their juices, about 8 more minutes. Then add the broth several ladles at a time, cooking while stirring continuously until the broth becomes a bit absorbed by the rice, adding more stock as needed until the rice is al dente (still has some bite and is not mushy) and creamy but not runny. Remove from heat and stir in cheese fully until melted. Serve with good bread and wine.

Mushrooms are extremely comforting in risotto, but this dish does not contain any carotene so it should be accompanied by carrots or other carotene source to protect the sulfur if experiencing metabolic disease. Tea should also be used to prevent fat saponification and microbial ammonia production.

Pizza

Dough

3 ½ cups flour
1 1/2 cups water
1/2 tsp salt
3 tablespoons olive oil
1 tsp dry active yeast

Mix ingredients together then knead until smooth, cover and allow to rise for at least 3 hours (longer rise results in better tasting crust). When ready to make pizza, preheat oven to 450°F (230°C), using a baking stone if you have one. Prepare sauce and toppings, then oil a baking sheet and spread dough to edges, top with sauce and toppings, then bake for 20-25 minutes until crust starts to brown (do not brown cheese much). If you don't have a baking stone, remove pizza from oven and place atop two burners on medium heat for 8 minutes to crisp up the bottom.

Traditional Red Sauce Pizza

1 can tomato purée (14-16 oz total)
1 tbsp olive oil
4-6 cloves garlic, minced
1 tsp salt
1 tsp fresh oregano, diced (dried is fine)

Sauce: Sauté garlic in olive oil over medium-low heat for 5 minutes. Add tomato, salt, and oregano and cook over medium about 10 minutes until it's less wet.

Toppings:
1 tbsp fresh basil, chiffonade
14-18 oz good mozzarella, shredded
optional: sliced fresh tomatoes, good pepperoni, sausage, sliced or diced mushrooms, olives, green peppers, etc.

Dandelion Greens and Pesto

Sauce: Pesto (page 38 or store-bought)

Toppings:
Bunch of dandelion greens, chopped
Extra basil
1 large shallot, julienned
3 medium, high quality tomatoes, sliced thinly
10 oz good goat cheese

Chicken with White Sauce

4 tablespoons butter
4-6 cloves garlic, minced
1 tsp black pepper
2 tablespoons flour
1 ½ cups whole milk
1 tsp sea salt
3 oz finely grated parmesan

Sauce: Sauté garlic in butter over medium-low heat for 5 minutes. Whisk in the flour and pepper and cook for 2 minutes, then whisk in the milk, and parmesan and cook until sauce thickens.

Toppings;
1-2 cups roast chicken meat, shredded
2 shallots, julienned (optional)
14-18 oz good mozzarella

Pizza is actually a very healthy food. Tomato puree is high in carotene and potassium, high-quality cheese is high in calcium, phosphorus, and B vitamins, the yeast-risen dough contributes more B vitamins, olive oil is high in oleic acid, etc.

Tortillas

3 cups flour (spelt, einkorn, kamut)
1 tsp baking powder
½ tsp salt
1 cup hot tap water
¼ cup olive oil, coconut oil, or high-oleic sunflower oil

Mix dry ingredients in a medium bowl, then add water and oil and mix until well combined and the dough is no longer sticky. Turn onto a counter and knead until dough is smooth but not overworked. Allow to sit, covered, 10-15 minutes. Then, heat a large pan on medium-high, and cut dough into 8-10 equal pieces, roll each into a ball, then flatten into a disc and set aside. When the pan has been hot for several minutes (but not smoking), lightly flour the work surface and roll each piece large and flat, flouring the dough to prevent sticking to the roller, then plop into hot pan. When large bubbles start to form (about 30 seconds) flip tortilla, and cook another 45 seconds on the other side, which will also puff up. Transfer to a plate and repeat with remaining dough.

Homemade, warm tortillas are extremely delicious. It can be tricky to place tortillas in the hot pan without accidentally folding them, however, and the trick is to let it drop in like a parachute, letting air keep it spread out. You will mess up but practice will make you better. Use for burritos, breakfast burritos, quesadillas, wraps, etc. Use refried beans (page 92), or fajita filling (page 66), or top with cheese and broil under a hot broiler for 5 minutes to accompany tomato soup (page 138).

Pot Pie

2X pie dough (below)
2 lb potatoes, peeled and cubed
1 lb of carrots, peeled and cubed
4-5 leeks, cleaned and chopped
1 tbsp salt
1 tbsp ground black pepper
6-7 bay leaves
¼ cup flour

1 cup heavy cream
2 cups stock
1 can cannellini beans
1 lb fresh green beans, chopped
1 package (16 oz) green peas
¼ cup fresh thyme, chopped
1 cup fresh parsley, chopped
3 egg yolks, scrambled

In a large pot over medium heat, melt the butter and sauté potatoes, carrots, leeks, salt, pepper, and bay leaves until soft but not mushy. Add the flour, mix, and cook for a few minutes before adding the stock, half and half, canelinis, thyme, and parsley. Cook until it comes to a boil and thickens, remove from heat and mix in the green beans, peas, thyme, and parsley, and allow to cool. As the filling cools prepare a pie dough as described on page 150, doubling the recipe, let rest, covered, for at least 30 minutes.

Preheat oven to 425°F (200°C), roll dough into two sheets (one larger than the other) using the larger to cover a 9x13 inch casserole pan. Brush the bottom layer of dough with thin egg wash to prevent soggy dough, then mix remaining eggs into filling before pouring it into pie, slightly mounded in the middle. Top with second dough sheet, crimp edges, poke the top with a fork for steam vents, then bake for 1 hour or until the crust is golden brown. Allow to rest for 10 minutes before serving.

Pie Dough

2 cups flour
12 tbsp cold butter
1 tsp salt
1-2 tbsp cold water

Like quiche, pot pie is a bit of work but exceptionally delicious and worth the effort. Change up the ingredients for interesting variations.

Make the dough by mixing the flour, butter, and salt together using a pastry cutter or dough mixer until it forms pea-size clumps and no fine flour remains. Sprinkle only enough of the cold water until the dough easily comes together. Form into a ball and let rest for at least 15 minutes before rolling.

A special thank you to my lovely supporters and patrons, without whom this book would not have been possible.

www.fuckportioncontrol.com